THE MOST POPULAR SUBROUTINES IN BASIC
BY KEN TRACTON

TAB BOOKS
BLUE RIDGE SUMMIT, PA. 17214

FIRST EDITION

FIRST PRINTING—JANUARY 1980

Copyright © 1980 by TAB BOOKS

Printed in the United States of America

Library of Congress Cataloging in Publication Data

Tracton, Ken.
    The most popular subroutines in BASIC.

    Includes index.
    1.   Basic (Computer program language)   I.   Title.
QA76.73.B3T73   001.6*425   79-16891
ISBN 0-8306-9740-3
ISBN 0-8306-1050-2 pbk.

Preface

The concept of the SUBROUTINE is used extensively in many computer languages under aliases such as procedures, modules, and functions.

In BASIC language the term subroutine is generally used to describe a function that can be repeated or called from the same program any number of times.

The scope of this text is oriented towards all users of BASIC, whether you are a professional or a hobbyist.

Chapter 1 covers the subroutine concept. Chapters 2-16 presents many popular subroutine listings. The full-scale programs provided in chapter 17 demonstrate the versatility of subroutines.

I would sincerely like to thank Mr. Alec Grynspan who took the time and effort to help me evaluate the subroutines and assist me in testing the sample programs.

All of the subroutines have been tested on a CDC-CYBER computer. Of course, the subroutines will run on all floating-point BASIC interpreters or compilers resident in any machine.

Ken Tracton

Contents

4 Degrees, Grads and Radians 73

5 Electronics 79

6 Graphs...89

Chapter 1
What Is A Subroutine?

BASIC has different types of statements such as:
- —DIM for dimensioning variables.
- —LET for assigning values and the results of calculations.
- —IF for making conditional branches and decisions.
- —GOTO for making unconditional branches.
- —END or STOP to stop running a program.
- —PRINT to output results.
- —INPUT to get values.
- —READ to accept DATA.
- —DATA to define values.
- —GOSUB and RETURN to control subroutines.

All the above examples can be thought of as building blocks or the bricks and lumber of a building. A subroutine is a module, as in modular or prefabricated construction. It can be combined with other modules and statements to build a program.

Like a building module, a subroutine is prepared once and simply duplicated where needed. An example would be a standardized door frame used throughout the building. Unlike a building, a subroutine is only built (written) once and then it is duplicated by the use of the GOSUB statement.

Since you always want to tell the computer when a subroutine is finished and the rest of the program is to continue, use a return statement. This statement tells the computer to continue processing at the statement following the GOSUB which called the subroutine. See Fig. 1-1. A subroutine can call other subroutines just as a door frame assembly consists of a separate door and frame. See Fig. 1-2.

HOW TO USE THIS BOOK

Most of the subroutines in this book have been carefully designed to be less than 10 lines long. All the routines are numbered consecutively in steps of 10 except for the REM (remark statement) identifying the routine which is numbered in single steps up to five.

When you want to include a subroutine in your program simply renumber the subroutine by increasing the line count. In the following example, 5 becomes 55 and 10 becomed 60—and so on.

The Subroutine
```
 5 REM SAMPLE SUBROUTINE
10 LET A=A1/(A1*A1+B1*B1)
20 LET B=−B1/(A1*A1+B1*B1)
30 RETURN
```

The Revised Subroutine
```
55 REM SAMPLE SUBROUTINE
60 LET A=A1/(A1*A1+B1*B1)
70 LET B=−B1/(A1*A1+B1*B1)
80 RETURN
```

Each subroutine includes input variables which are used in the calculations the programmer or program must set prior to calling the subroutine and their meanings. Working variables are used by the subroutine as a kind of temporary storage area. Output variables are the results of the calculations and their meanings.

REMEMBER THESE RULES
- Set your input variables before you issue the GOSUB.
- Altered variables will probably contain *garbage* upon return.
- Do not change the output variables before you use them.

VARIABLES NAMES

Because of the way variables and subroutines are handled in BASIC you might find that there is a conflict in variable names used in this book and the names you might want to use.

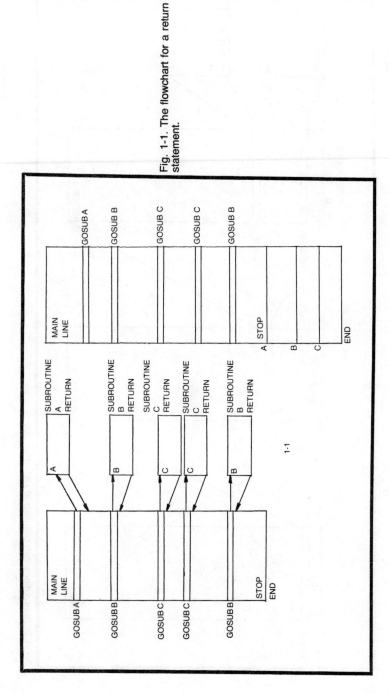

Fig. 1-1. The flowchart for a return statement.

11

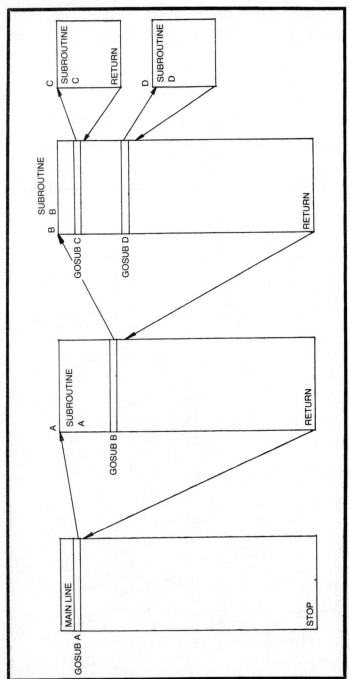

Fig. 1-2. Subroutines can be used to call other subroutines.

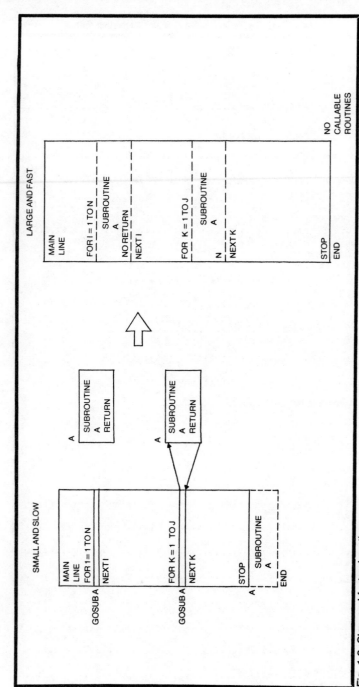

Fig. 1-3. Slow and fast subroutines.

13

Table 1-1. The Typical Subroutine Documentation Form.

SUBROUTINE DOCUMENTATION

SUBROUTINE DESCRIPTION . . . .

WRITTEN BY . . . .

DATE WRITTEN . . . . DATE CHECKED . . . .

PURPOSE . . . .

. . . .

. . . .

    INPUT VARIABLES . . . .

                . . . .

                . . . .

    OUTPUT VARIABLES . . . .

                . . . .

                . . . .

    WORKING VARIABLES . . . .

                . . . .

    SUBROUTINE LISTING . . . .

. . . .

. . . .

. . . .

. . . .

. . . .

. . . .

. . . .

. . . .

. . . .

If this does occur, change the variable name in the subroutine, *wherever* it occurs, to the name you want to use. In the following example, C and D are substituted for X and Y.

The Subroutine
```
 5 REM SAMPLE ROUTINE
10 LET X=X*X/5.4*Y
20 RETURN
```

The Revised Subroutine
```
 5 REM SAMPLE ROUTINE
10 LET C=C*C/5.4*D
20 RETURN
```

INLINE SUBSTITUTION FOR EFFICIENT CODING

If you have used the previously mentioned techniques to adapt your subroutine, it should work very nicely. However, you might want to perform what is commonly called a *space-time-trade-off* to make your program run faster.

You can do this this quite easily if you convert the subroutine to an *in-line* routine. Remove both the GOSUB statement from the program you are writing and the RETURN from the subroutine. Place the remainder of the subroutine into the position previously occupied by the GOSUB. Repeat the process with each GOSUB.

You will find that you program runs much faster—particularly if the GOSUB statements are inside a heavily used loop. However, this program does use considerably more space (Fig. 1-3).

Because each copy is independent of the others, you can tune the variable names. *Remember* that subroutines are building blocks for your programming and you can manipulate them as you wish.

An observant reader will notice that the subroutines are, on the average, very short. The reason for this is quite simple. This book gives you the most widely used and useful subroutines and functions. You will have the materials to write large programs by combining the appropriate subroutines.

In addition, this book provides a series of full-scale programs which show the use of some of the subroutines provided and subroutines in general.

All the subroutines in this book are documented using a standard layout (Table 1-1). When you write your own subroutines you can use a similar layout. Type up a few of these as a reminder and use the format consistently.

Chapter 2
Annuities and Compound Amounts

This section gives the routines most used to calculate values used in loans, mortgages, trust funds and annuities. Routines are given to solve for:

- —future value—from a known present value.
- —interest—total interest accumulated.
- —interest rates.
- —present value—for a desired future value.
- —time periods—the time required to give the desired future value from a present value that is also given.

Given any four of the above, you can solve the fifth with these subroutines.

FUTURE VALUE

Purpose: Computes future value based on a present value.

Variables needed: Y (present value). I (interest rate). N (time periods).

Variables altered: None.

Variables returned: X (future value).

Equations: $X = Y(1+I)^N$

Source:
```
 5 REM
10 LET X=Y*(1+I) ↑ N
20 RETURN
```

Test Run For Future Value

```
RUN
INPUT VARIABLES:
2000,.1,12
25000,.1,12
2000,.1,24
25000,.1,24
2000,.1,36
RESULTS:
INPUT        OUTPUT
2000,.1,12   6276.8568
25000,.1,12  78460.709
2000,.1,24   19699.465
25000,.1,24  246243.32
2000,.1,36   61825.361
RUN COMPLETE
END*
```

INTEREST

Purpose: Computes accumulated compound interest.

Variables needed: Y (present value). I (interest rate). N (time periods).

Variables altered: None.

Variables returned: A (interest).

Equations: $A = Y((1+I)^N - 1)$

Source:
```
 5 REM COMPUTES INTEREST
10 LET A = Y*(((1+I) ↑ N)-1)
20 RETURN
```

Test Run For Interest

```
RUN
INPUT VARIABLES:
2000,.1,12
25000,.1,12
2000,.1,24
25000,.1,24
2000,.1,36

RESULTS:
INPUT        OUTPUT
2000,.1,12   4276.8568
25000,.1,12  53460.709
2000,.1,24   17699.465
25000,.1,24  221243.32
2000,.1,36   59825.361
RUN COMPLETE
END*
```

INTEREST RATE

Purpose: Computes interest rate for a given future value.

Variables needed: X (future value). Y (present value). N (time periods).

Variables altered: None.

Variables returned: I (interest rate).

Equations: $I=((X/Y)^{1/N}-1$

Source:

```
5 REM COMPUTES INTEREST RATE
10 LET I=((CX/Y)↑(1N))-1
20 RETURN
```

Test Run For Interest Rate

```
RUN
INPUT VARIABLES:
?6276.8568,2000,12
?78460.709,25000,12
?19699.465,2000,24
?246243.32,25000,24
?61825.361,2000,36
RESULTS:
```

INPUT	OUTPUT
6276.8568,2000,12	0.1
78460.709,25000,12	0.1
19699.465,2000,24	0.1
246243.32,25000,24	0.1
61825.361,2000,36	0.1

```
RUN COMPLETE
END*
```

PRESENT VALUE

Purpose: Computes the present value based on a future value.

Variables needed: X (future value). I (interest rate). N (time periods).

Variables altered: None.

Variables returned: Y (present value).

Equations: $Y=X(1+I)^{-N}$

Source:

```
5 REM COMPUTES PRESENT VALUE
10 LET Y=X*(1+I)↑(-N)
20 RETURN
```

Test Run For Present Value

```
RUN
INPUT VARIABLES:
?6276.8568,.1,12
?78460.709,.1,12
?19699.465,.1,24
?246243.32,.1,24
?61825.361,.1,36
RESULTS:
OUTPUT
2000
25000
2000
25000
2000
RUN COMPLETE
END*
```

TIME PERIODS

Purpose: Computes the number of time periods from the present value to the future value.

Variables needed: X (future value). Y (present value). I (interest rate).

Variables altered: None.

Variables returned: N (time periods).

Equations: $N = \dfrac{\ln(X/Y)}{\ln(1+I)}$

Source:

```
 5 REM COMPUTES TIME PERIODS
10 LET N = (LOG(X/Y))/(LOG(1+I))
20 RETURN
```

Test Run For Time Periods

```
RUN
INPUT VARIABLES:
?2000, 6276.8568,.1
?25000,78460.709,.1
?2000,19699.465,.1
?25000,246243.32,.1

RESULTS:
OUTPUT
12
12
24
24
36
RUN COMPLETE
END*
```

Chapter 3
Conversions

Data is often supplied in conflicting units of measure and has to be changed to standard units in order to be used in calculations. For example:

- —air conditioners are rated in BTU per day.
- —heat flow is measured in calories per second.
- —energy is measured in joules.
- —electrical power is measured in watts.
- —electrical energy is measured in watt-seconds.
- —motor capacities are measured in horsepower.

This book contains the most frequently used conversions in the fields of chemistry, physics, mathematics and mechanics. Special attention has been paid to conversions useful to electronic professionals and hobbyists. The formulas given here are stated as relationships and not as expressions. The expression: $A=.5J$ means that A is equivalent to one half of J. The relationship: $A=.5J$ means that when you multiply the units of J by .5 gives A. In other words, inches=12 feet means that a 6 foot length multiplied by 12 gives 72 inches.

ACRE-FEET

Purpose: To compute acre-feet (aft.) from cubic meters (m^3).
Variables needed: M (cubic meters).
Variables altered: None.
Variables returned: A (acre-feet).
Equations: aft equals $8.107 \times 10^{-4} m^3$
Source:

```
 5 REM ACRE-FEET
10 LET A=8.107E-04*M
20 RETURN
```

Test Run For Subroutine Acre Feet

```
RUN
INPUT VARIABLES:
?1
?2
?3
?4
?5
RESULTS:
OUTPUT
8.107E-04
1.6214E-03
2.4321E-03
2.2428E-03
4.0535E-03
RUNCOMPLETE
END*
```

Angstrom Units

Purpose: To compute angstrom units (Å) from nanometers (nm).

Variables needed: N (nm).

Variables altered: None.

Variables returned: A (Å).

Equations: Å equals 10 nm.

Source:.

```
 5 REM ANSTROM UNITS
10 LET A=10*N
20 RETURN
```

BARRELS

Purpose: To compute barrels (bb) from cubic meters (m3).

Variables needed: M (cubic meters).

Variables altered: None.

Variables returned: B (barrels).

Equations: bbl 6.2893 m^3

Source:

```
 5 REM BARRELS
10 LET B=6.2893*M
20 RETURN
```

Test Run For Barrels

```
RUN
INPUT VARIABLES:
?1
?2
```

?3
?4
?5
RESULTS:
OUTPUT
6.2893000
12.578600
18.867900
25.157200
31.446500
RUN COMPLETE
END*

BRITISH THERMAL UNITS (BTU)

Purpose: To compute BTU from joules.
Variables needed: J (joules).
Variables altered: None.
Variables returned: B (BTU).
Equation: BTU equals $9.4787 \times 10^{-4} j$
Source:

```
 5 REM BTU
10 LET B=9.4787E-04*J
20 RETURN
```

Test Run For BTU

RUN
INPUT VARIABLES:
?1
?2
?3
?4
?5
RESULTS:
OUTPUT
9.4787E-04
1.89574E-03
2.84361E-03
3.79148E-03
4.73935E-03
RUN COMPLETE
END*

BTU/HR

Purpose: To compute BTU/Hr from watts.
Variables needed: W (watts).
Variables altered: None.
Variables returned: B (BTU/Hr).
Equation: BTU/Hr equals 3.1412 watts
Source:

```
 5 REM BTU/HR
10 LET B=3.1412*W
20 RETURN
```

Test Run For Subroutine BTU/HR

```
RUN
INPUT VARIABLES:
?1
?2
?3
?3
?4
?5
RESULTS:
OUTPUT
3.1412000
6.2824000
9.4236000
12.564800
15.706000
RUN COMPLETE
END*
```

CALORIES (THERMO-CHEMICAL)

Purpose: To compute calories from joules.

Variables Needed: J (joules).

Variables altered: None.

Variables returned: C (calories).

Equation: Cal equal $0.239j$

Source:
```
 5 REM CALORIES
10 LET C=0.239*J
20 RETURN
```

Test Run For Calories

```
RUN
INPUT VARIABLES:
?1
?2
?3
?4
?5
RESULTS:
OUTPUT
0.2390000
0.4780000
0.7170000
0.9560000
1.1950000
RUN COMPLETE
END*
```

CANDELAS PER SQUARE METER

Purpose: To compute candelas per square meter from foot-lambers (cd/m² from fL).

Variables needed: F (fL).

Variables altered: None.

Variables returned: C (cd/m²).

Equations: cd/m^2 equals 3.426 fL

Source:

```
5 REM CANDELAS/SQUARE METER
10 LET C=3.426*F
20 RETURN
```

Test Run For Subroutine Candelas Per Square Meter

```
RUN
INPUT VARIABLES:
?1
?2
?3
·?4
?5
RESULTS:
OUTPUT
3.426000
6.8520000
10.278000
13.704000
17.130000
RUN COMPLETE
END*
```

CELSIUS (DEGREE TEMPERATURE)

Purpose: To compute °Celsius (°C) from degrees Fahrenheit (°F).

Variables needed: F (°F).

Variables altered: None.

Variables returned: C (°C).

Equations: °C equals 0.55556 (°F-32)

Source:

```
5 REM CELSIUS
10 LET C=0.55556*(F-32)
20 RETURN
```

Test Run For Celsius

```
RUN
INPUT VARIABLES:
?98.6
?212
?0
?100
?-40
RESULTS:
OUTPUT
37
100
-17.777778
37.7777778
-40
RUN COMPLETE
END*
```

24

CENTIMETERS

Purpose: To compute centimeters (cm) from feet (ft).
Variables needed: F (ft).
Variables altered: None.
Variables returned: C (cm).
Equations: cm equals 30.48 ft
Source:
```
 5 REM CENTIMETERS
10 LET C=30.48*F
20 RETURN
```

Test Run For Centimeters/Feet
```
RUN
INPUT VARIABLES:
?1
?2
?3
?4
?5
RESULTS:
OUTPUT
30.480000
60.960000
91.440000
121.92000
152.40000
RUN COMPLETE
END*
```

CUBIC CENTIMETERS

Purpose: To compute cubic centimeters (cm^3) from cubic inches (in^3).
Variables needed: I (in^3):
Variables altered: None.
Variables returned: C (cm^3).
Equations: cm^3
Source:
```
 5 REM CUBIC CENTIMETERS
10 LET C =16.39*I
20 RETURN
```

Test Run For Cubic Centimeters/Inches
```
RUN
INPUT VARIABLES:
?1
?2
?3
```

?4
?5
RESULTS;
OUTPUT
16.390000
32.780000
49.170000
65.560000
81.950000
RUN COMPLETE
END*

CUBIC FEET

Purpose: To compute cubic feet (ft³) from cubic meters (m³).
Variables needed: M (cubic meters).
Variables altered: None.
Variables returned: F (cubic feet).
Equations: ft³ equals 35.31 m³
Source:

```
 5 REM CUBIC FEET
10 LET F=35.31*M
20 RETURN
```

Test Run For Cubic Feet/Meters

RUN
INPUT VARIABLES:
?1
?2
?3
?4
?5
RESULTS:
OUTPUT
35.310000
70.620000
105.93000
141.24000
176.55000
RUN COMPLETE
END*

CUBIC INCHES

Purpose: To compute cubic inches (in³) from cubic centimeters (cm³).
Variables needed: C (cm³).
Variables altered: None.
Variables returned: I (in³).
Equations: in³ equals 6.10128×10^{-2} cm³
Source:

```
5 REM CUBIC INCHES
10 LET I=6.10128E-02*C
20 RETURN
```

Test Run For Cubic Inches/Centimeters

```
RUN
INPUT VARIABLES:
?1
?2
?3
?4
?5
RESULTS:
OUTPUT
6.10128E-02
0.1220256
1.830384E-01
2.440512E-01
3.050640E-01
RUN COMPLETE
END*
```

CUBIC METERS

Purpose: To compute cubic meters (m^3) from cubic feet (ft^3).
Variables needed: F (cubic feet).
Variables altered: None.
Variables returned: M (cubic meters).
Equations: M^3 equals $0.02832\ ft^3$
Source:
```
5 REM CUBIC METERS
10 LET M=0.02832*F
20 RETURN
```

Test Run For Cubic Meter/Feet

```
RUN
INPUT VARIABLES:
?1
?2
?3
?4
?5
?6
?7
?8
?9
?10
RESULTS:
OUTPUT
2.832E-02
5.664E-02
8.496E-02
0.1132800
```

27

```
0.1416000
0.1699200
0.1982400
0.2265600
0.2548800
0.2832000
RUN COMPLETE
END*
```

CUBIC YARDS

Purpose: To compute cubic yards (yd³) from cubic meters (m³).

Variables needed: M (cubic meters).

Variables altered: None.

Variables returned: Y (cubic yards).

Equations: yd³ equals 1.3079 m³

Source:

```
 5 REM CUBIC YARDS
10 LET Y=1.3079*M
20 RETURN
```

Test Run For Cubic Yards/Meters

```
RUN
INPUT VARIABLES:
?1
?2
?3
?4
?5
?6
?7
?8
?9
?10
RESULTS:
OUTPUT
INPUT   OUTPUT
1       1.3079000
2       2.6158000
3       3.927000
4       5.2316000
5       6.5395000
6       7.8474000
7       9.1553000
8       10.463200
9       11.771100
10      13.079000
RUN COMPLETE
END*
```

DYNES

Purpose: To compute dynes (dyn) from newtons (N).
Variables needed: N (N).

Variables altered: None.
Variables returned: D (dyn).
Equation: D equals 1×10^5 N
Source:

```
5 REM DYNES
10 LET D=1E5*N
20 RETURN
```

Test Run For Dynes/Newtons

```
RUN
INPUT VARIABLES:
?1
?2
?3
?4
?5
?6
?7
?8
?9
?10
RESULTS
OUTPUT
```

OUTPUT	INPUT
100000.00	1
200000.00	2
300000.00	3
400000.00	4
500000.00	5
600000.00	6
700000.00	7
800000.00	8
900000.00	9
1.0E06	10

```
RUN COMPLETE
END*
```

FAHRENHEIT (DEGREES TEMPERATURE)

Purpose: To compute °Fahrenheit from °Celsius.
Variables needed: C (°C).
Variables altered: None.
Variables returned: F (°F).
Equations: °F equal $1.8°C + 32$
Source:

```
5 REM FAHRENHEIT
10 LET E=1.8*C+32
20 RETURN
```

Test Run For Fahrenheit/Celsius

```
RUN
INPUT VARIABLES:
?-40
?-20
?-10
?-5
?0
?10
?20
?30
?37
?50
?100
RESULTS:
OUTPUT
INPUT     OUTPUT
-40       -40.000000
-20       -4.0000000
-10       14.000000
-5        23.000000
0         32.000000
10        50.000000
20        68.000000
30        86.000000
37        98.600000
50        122.00000
100       212.00000
RUN COMPLETE
END*
```

FEET

Purpose: To compute feet (ft) from centimeters (cm).
Variables needed: C (cm).
Variables altered: None.
Variables returned: F (ft).
Equations: ft equals 3.2808×10^{-2} cm
Source:
```
5 REM FEET
10 LET F=3.2808E-02*C
20 RETURN
```

Test Run For Feet/CM

```
RUN
INPUT VARIABLES:
?1
?2
?3
?4
?5
?6
```

```
?7
?8
?9
?10
?20
?30
?40
?50
?100
RESULTS:
OUTPUT

INPUT    OUTPUT
1        3.2808E-02
2        6.5616E-02
3        9.8425E-02
4        0.1312300
5        0.1640400
6        0.1968500
7        0.2296500
8        0.2624600
9        0.2952800
10       0.3280800
20       0.6561600
30       0.9842500
40       1.3123000
50       1.6404000
100      3.2808000
RUN COMPLETE
END*
```

FLUID OUNCES (U.S.)

Purpose: To compute U.S. fluid ounces (oz) from milliliters (ml).
Variables needed: M (ml).
Variables altered: None.
Variables returned: Z (oz.)
Equations: oz equals 3.3818×10^{-2} ml
Source:
```
 5 REM FLUID OUNCES (U.S.)
10 LET Z=3.3818E-02*M
20 RETURN
```

Test Run For Fluid Ounces (U.S.)
```
RUN
INPUT VARIABLES:

?1
?2
?4
?8
?16
```

```
?32
?64
?128
?256
?512
?1024
?2048
?4096
RESULTS:
OUTPUT
INPUT    OUTPUT
1        3.3818E-02
2        6.7636E-02
4        0.1352720
8        0.2705440
16       0.5410880
32       1.0821760
64       2.1643520
128      4.3287040
256      8.6574080
512      17.314816
1024     34.629632
2048     69.259264
4096     138.51853
RUN COMPLETE
END*
```

FOOT-CANDLES

Purpose: To compute foot-candles (fc) from LUX (Lx).
Variables needed: L (LUX).
Variables altered: None.
Variables returned: F (fc).
Equations: fc equals 9.294×10^{-2} LUX

Source:
```
5 REM FOOT-CANDLES
10 LET F=9.294E-02*L
20 RETURN
```

Test Run For Foot-Candles

```
RUN
INPUT VARIABLES:
?1
?2
?4
?8
?16
?32
?64
?128
?256
?512
?1024
```

```
?2048
?4096
RESULTS:
OUTPUT
INPUT    OUTPUT
1        9.294E-02
2        0.1858800
4        0.3717600
8        0.7435200
16       1.4870400
32       2.9740800
64       5.9481600
128      11.896320
256      23.792640
512      47.585280
1024     95.170560
2048     190.34112
4096     380.68224
RUN COMPLETE
END*
```

FOOT-POUNDS FORCE PER SECOND

Purpose: To compute the ft-lb f/s from watts.
Variables needed: W (watts).
Variables altered: None.
Variables returned: F (foot-pounds force per second).
Equations: ft-lb-f/s equals 0.7375 watts
Sources:

```
5 REM FOOT-POUNDS/SECOND
10 LET F=0.7375*W
20 RETURN
```

Test Run For Foot-Pounds-Force Per Second
```
RUN
INPUT VARIABLES:
?.75
?1.5
?3.0
?6
?12
?24
?48
?96
?192
?384
?768
RESULTS:
OUTPUT
INPUT    OUTPUT
.75      0.5531250
1.5      1.1062500
3        2.2125000
```

6	4.4250000
12	8.8500000
24	17.700000
48	35.400000
96	70.800000
192	141.60000
384	283.20000
768	566.40000

RUN COMPLETE
END*

GALLONS (U.S.)

Purpose: To compute gallons (gal) from liters (1).
Variables needed: L (1).
Variables altered: None.
Variables returned: G (gal).
Equations: gal equals 0.2642 1
Source:

```
 5 REM GALLONS ( U.S.)
10 LET G=0.2642*L
20 RETURN
```

Test Run For Gallons (U.S.)

RUN
INPUT VARIABLES:
?.1
?.3
?.9
?2.7
?8.1
?24.3
?72.9
?218.7
?656.1
?1968.3
?5904.9
RESULTS:
OUTPUT

INPUT	OUTPUT
.1	2.642E-02
.3	7.926E-02
.9	0.2377800
2.7	2.1400200
24.3	6.4200600
72.9	19.260180
218.7	57.780540
656.1	173.34162
1968.3	520.02486
5904.9	1560.0746

RUN COMPLETE
END*

GRAMS

Purpose: To compute grams (gm) from ounces (oz avdp-ounces).

Variables needed: Z (ounces).

Variables altered: None.

Variables returned: G (grams).

Equations: gm equals 28.35 oz.

Source:

```
 5 REM GRAMS
10 LET G=28.35*Z
20 RETURN
```

Test Run For Grams

```
RUN
INPUT VARIABLES:
?.1
?.2
?.4
?.8
?1.6
?3.2
?6.4
?12.8
?.25.6
?51.2
?102.4
RESULTS:
OUTPUT
```

INPUT	OUTPUT
.1	2.8350000
.2	5.6700000
.4	11.340000
.8	22.680000
1.6	45.360000
3.2	90.720000
6.4	181.44000
12.8	362.88000
25.6	725.76000
51.2	1451.52000
102.4	2903.0400

```
RUN COMPLETE
END*
```

HORSEPOWER (ELECTRICAL)

Purpose: To compute the amount of horsepower produced by X watts.

Variables needed: W (watts).

Variables altered: None.

Variables returned: H (HP).

Equations: HP equals 1.3405×10^{-3} watts

Source:
```
 5 REM HP
10 LET H=1.3405E-03*W
20 RETURN
```

Test Run For Horsepower

```
RUN
INPUT VARIABLES:
?1
?10
?20
?40
?100
?250
?500
?1000
?2000
?75
RESULTS:
OUTPUT
INPUT    OUTPUT
1        1.3405E-03
10       1.3405E-02
20       2.681E-02
40       5.362E-02
100      1.3405000
250      0.3351250
500      0.6702500
1000     1.3405000
2000     2.6810000
75       0.1005375
RUN COMPLETE
END*
```

INCHES

Purpose: To compute inches (in) from millimeters (mm).
Variables needed: M (mm).
Variables altered: None.
Variables returned: I (in).
Equations: in equals 3.937×10^{-2} mm

Source:
```
 5 REM INCHES
10 LET I=3.937E-02*M
20 RETURN
```

Test Run For Subroutine Inches

```
RUN
INPUT VARIABLES:
```

```
?1
?25.4
?304.8
?2
?8
?12
?17
?19
?22
?64
?1.6
RESULTS:
OUTPUT
INPUT    OUTPUT
1        3.937E-02
25.4     0.9999998
304.8    11.999976
2        7.874E-02
8        0.3149600
12       0.4724400
17       0.6692900
19       0.7480300
22       0.8661400
16       0.6299200
64       2.5196800
1.6      0.0417322
RUN COMPLETE
END*
```

JOULES

Purpose: To compute joules from BTU (British Thermal Units).

Variables needed: B (BTU)

Variables altered: None.

Variables returned: J (joules).

Equations: J equals 1055BTU

Source:

```
5 REM JOULES
10 LET J=1055*B
20 RETURN
```

Test Run For Joules/BTU

```
RUN
INPUT VARIABLES:
?.01
?.02
?.04
?.1
?.2
?1
?1.5
?1.7
```

```
?1.9
?1.8
?.1.1
RESULTS:
OUTPUT
INPUT    OUTPUT
.01      10.550000
.02      21.100000
.04      42.200000
.1       105.50000
.2       211.00000
1        1055.0000
1.5      1582.5000
1.7      1793.5000
1.9      2004.5000
1.8      1899.0000
1.1      1160.5000
RUN COMPLETE
END*
```

JOULES

Purpose: To compute joules from calories (thermo-chemical).
Variables needed: C (calories).
Variables altered: None.
Variables returned: J (joules).
Equation: j equals 4.184Cal
Source:

```
 5 REM JOULES
10 LET J=4.184*C
20 RETURN
```

Test Run For Joules/Calories

```
RUN
INPUT VARIABLES:
?1
?7
?49
?2
?4
?8
?16
?3
?9
?27
?81
RESULTS:
OUTPUT
INPUT    OUTPUT
1        4.1840000
7        29.288000
49       205.01600
2        8.3680000
```

4	16.736000
8	33.472000
16	66.944000
3	12.552000
9	37.656000
27	112.96800
81	225.93600

RUN COMPLETE
END*

JOULES

Purpose: To compute joules from foot-pounds force.
Variables needed: F (foot-pounds force).
Variables altered: None.
Variables returned: J (joules)
Equation: joules equal 1.356ft-lb-f
Source:

```
5 REM JOULES
10 LET J=1.356*F
20 RETURN
```

Test Run For Joules/Foot-Pounds

```
RUN
INPUT VARIABLES:
?4096
?1
?2048
?2
?1024
?4
?512
?8
?256
?16
?128
RESULTS:
OUTPUT
```

INPUT	OUTPUT
4096	5554.1760
1	1.3560000
2048	2777.0880
2	2.7120000
1024	1388.5440
4	5.4240000
512	694.27200
8	10.848000
256	347.13600
16	21.696000
128	173.56800

RUN COMPLETE
END*

KILOGRAMS

Purpose: To compute kilograms (Kg) from pounds (lb).
Variables needed: P (pounds).
Variables altered: None.
Variables returned: K (kilograms).
Equations: Kg equals 0.4536 lb
Source:

```
 5 REM KILOGRAMS
10 LET K=0.4536*P
20 RETURN
```

Test Run For Kilograms/Pound
```
RUN
INPUT VARIABLES:
?1
?2
?3
?4
?2000
?700
?1300
?1700
?1900
?420
RESULTS:
OUTPUT
```

INPUT	OUTPUT
1	.45360000
2	.90720000
3	1.3608000
4	1.8143700
2000	907.20000
700	317.52000
1300	589.67000
1700	771.10700
1900	861.82500
420	190.51000

```
RUN COMPLETE
END*
```

KILOGRAMS PER CUBIC METER

Purpose: To compute kilograms per cubic meter (Kg/m^3) from pounds per cubic foot (lb/ft^3).
Variables needed: P (lb/ft^3).
Variables altered: None.
Variables returned: K (Kg/m^3).
Equations: Kg/m^3 equals 16.02 lb/ft^3
Source:

```
5 REM KG/M↑3
10 LET K=16.02*P
20 RETURN
```

Test Run For Kilograms/Cubic Meter

```
RUN
INPUT VARIABLES:
?1
?2
?4
?8
?16
?32
?64
?128
?256
?3
?9
RESULTS:
OUTPUT
INPUT   OUTPUT
1       16.020000
2       32.040000
4       64.080000
8       128.16000
16      256.32000
32      512.64000
64      1025.2800
128     2050.5600
256     4101.1200
3       48.060000
9       144.18000
RUN COMPLETE
END*
```

KILOGRAMS PER SQUARE METER (Kg/m²)

Purpose: To compute Kg/m^2 from PASCALS (Pa).
Variables needed: P (Pa).
Variables altered: None.
Variables returned: K (Kg/m^2).
Equations: Kg/m^2 equals 0.10197 Pa
Source:

```
5 REM KILOGRAMS PER SQUARE METER
10 LET K=0.10197*P
20 RETURN
```

Test Run For Kilograms/Square Meter

```
RUN
INPUT VARIABLES:
?1
?5
```

```
?25
?125
?625
?2
?4
?8
?16
?32
?64
RESULTS:
OUTPUT
INPUT    OUTPUT
1        0.1019700
5        0.5098500
25       2.5492500
125      12.746250
625      63.731250
2        0.2039400
4        0.4078800
8        0.8157600
16       1.6315200
32       3.2630400
64       6.5260800
RUN COMPLETE
END*
```

KILOMETERS

Purpose: To compute kilometers (km) from nautical miles (nmi).

Variables needed: N (nmi).

Variables altered: None.

Variables returned: K (km).

Equations: km equals 1.852 nmi

Source:
```
 5 REM KILOMETERS
10 LET K=1.852*N
20 RETURN
```

Test Run For Kilometers/Nautical Miles
```
RUN
INPUT VARIABLES:
?5
?10
?15
?20
?25
?30
?35
?40
?80
?160
?320
RESULTS:
OUTPUT
```

INPUT	OUTPUT
5	9.2600000
10	18.520000
15	27.780000
20	37.040000
25	46.300000
30	55.560000
35	64.820000
40	74.080000
80	148.16000
160	296.32000
320	592.64000

RUN COMPLETE
END*

KILOMETERS

Purpose: To compute kilometers (km) from statute miles (mi).

Variables needed: M (mi).

Variables altered: None.

Variables returned: K (km).

Equations: km equals 1.609 mi

Source:

```
5 REM KILOMETERS
10 LET K=1.609*M
20 RETURN
```

Test Run For Kilometers/Miles

```
RUN
INPUT VARIABLES:
?5
?10
?15
?20
?25
?30
?35
?40
?80
?160
?320
RESULTS:
OUTPUT
```

INPUT	OUTPUT
5	8.0467200
10	16.093440
15	24.140160
20	32.186880
25	40.233600
30	48.280320
35	56.327040
40	64.373760

```
80      128.74752
160     257.49504
320     514.99008
RUN COMPLETE
END*
```

KILOMETERS PER HOUR

Purpose: To compute kilometers per hour (Km/Hr) from meters per second (m/s).

Variables needed: M (m/s).

Variables altered: None.

Variables returned: K (Km/Hr).

Equations: Km/Hr equals 3.5997 m/s

Source:

```
5 REM KPH
10 LET K=3.5997*M
20 RETURN
```

Test Run For Kilometers/Hour

```
RUN
INPUT VARIABLES:
?1
?2
?4
?8
?16
?32
?64
?128
?256
?3
?9
RESULTS:
OUTPUT
INPUT   OUTPUT
1       3.5997000
2       7.1994000
4       14.398800
8       28.797600
16      57.595200
32      115.19040
64      230.38080
128     460.76160
256     921.52320
3       10.799100
9       32.397300
RUN COMPLETE
END*
```

KILOPASCALS

Purpose: To compute kPa (kiloPascals) from lb/in²

Variables needed: P (lb/in²).

Variables altered: None.
Variables returned: K (kPa).
Equations: kPa equals 6.895 lb/in^2
Source:

```
5 REM KPA
10 LET K=6.895*P
20 RETURN
```

Test Run For Kilopascals

```
RUN
INPUT VARIABLES:

?1
?2
?3
?4
?5
?10
?20
?40
?80
?160
?320
RESULTS:
OUTPUT
INPUT   OUTPUT
  1     6.8950000
  2     13.790000
  3     20.685000
  4     27.580000
  5     34.475000
 10     68.950000
 20     137.90000
 40     275.80000
 80     551.60000
160     1103.2000
320     2206.4000
```

```
RUN COMPLETE
END*
```

KNOTS

Purpose: To compute knots (kn) from meters per second (m/s).

Variables needed: M (m/s).
Variables altered: None.
Variables returned: K (knots).
Equations: kn equals 1.944 m/s
Source:

```
 5 REM KNOTS
10 LET K=1.944*M
20 RETURN
```

Test Run For Knots

```
RUN
INPUT VARIABLES:
?10
?20
?30
?40
?50
?60
?70
?80
?90
?100
?110
RESULTS:
OUTPUT
INPUT   OUTPUT
10      19.440000
20      38.880000
30      58.320000
40      77.760000
50      97.200000
60      116.64000
70      136.08000
80      155.52000
90      174.96000
100     194.40000
110     213.84000
RUN COMPLETE
END*
```

LITERS

Purpose: To compute liters (1) from imperial gallons (gal).
Variables needed: G (gal).
Variables altered: None.
Variables returned: L (1).
Equations: 1 equals 4.546 gal
Source:

```
 5 REM LITERS
10 LET L=4.546*G
20 RETURN
```

Test Run For Liters/IMP

```
RUN
INPUT VARIABLES:
```

```
?0.22
?0.44
?1
?2
?3
?11
?15
?17
?24
?27
RESULTS:
OUTPUT
INPUT    OUTPUT
0.22     1.0002000
0.44     2.004000
1        4.5460000
2.       9.0920000
3        13.638000
11       50.010000
15       68.190000
17       77.290000
24       109.11000
27       122.75000
RUN COMPLETE
END*
```

LITERS

Purpose: To compute liters (1) from U.S. gallons (gal).
Variables needed: G (gal).
Variables altered: None.
Variables returned: L (1).
Equations: 1 equals 3.785 gal
Source:

```
 5 REM LITERS
10 LET L=3.785*G
20 RETURN
```

Test Run For Liters/U.S.

```
RUN
INPUT VARIABLES:
?1
?2
?4
?8
?16
?32
?64
?128
?256
?512
?1024
```

RESULTS:
OUTPUT

INPUT	OUTPUT
1	3.7850000
2	7.5700000
4	15.140000
8	30.280000
16	60.560000
32	121.12000
64	242.24000
128	484.48000
256	968.96000
512	1937.9200
1024	3875.8400

RUN COMPLETE
END*

METERS

Purpose: To compute meters (m) from yards (yd).
Variables needed: Y (yd).
Variables altered: None.
Variables returned: M (m).
Equations: m equals 0.9144 yd
Source:

```
5 REM METERS
10 LET M=0.9144*Y
20 RETURN
```

Test Run For Meters

RUN
INPUT VARIABLES:
?1
?10
?100
?1000
?1760
?50
?25
?5
?12.5
?2
?3.25
RESULTS:
OUTPUT

INPUT	OUTPUT
1	.91440000
10	9.1440000
100	91.440000
1000	914.40000
1760	1609.3440
50	45.720000
25	22.860000
5	4.5720000

12.5	11.430000
2	1.8288000
3.25	2.9718000

RUN COMPLETE
END*

METERS PER SECOND

Purpose: To compute meters per second (m/s) from kilometers per hour (Km/Hr).
Variables needed: K (Km/Hr).
Variables altered: None.
Variables returned: M (m/s).
Equations: m/s equals 0.2778 Km/Hr
Source:

```
 5 REM M/S
10 LET M=0.2778*K
20 RETURN
```

Test Run For Meters/Second (KM)

```
RUN
INPUT VARIABLES:
?1
?2
?4
?8
?16
?32
?64
?128
?256
?512
RESULTS:
OUTPUT
```

INPUT	OUTPUT
1	0.2778000
2	0.5556000
4	1.1112000
8	2.2224000
16	4.4448000
32	8.8896000
64	17.779200
128	35.558400
256	71.116800
512	142.23360

RUN COMPLETE
END*

METERS PER SECOND

Purpose: To compute meters per second (m/s) from knots (kn).

Variables needed: K (knots).
Variables altered: None.
Variables returned: M (m/s).
Equations: m/s equals 0.5144 kn
Source:

```
5 REM M/S
10 LET M=0.5144*K
20 RETURN
```

Test Run For Meters/Second (Knots)

```
RUN
INPUT VARIABLES
?1
?2
?4
?8
?16
?32
?64
?128
RESULTS:
OUTPUT
INPUT    OUTPUT
1        0.5144000
2        1.0288000
4        2.0576000
8        4.1152000
16       8.234000
32       16.460800
64       32.921600
128      65.843200
RUN COMPLETE
END*
```

METERS PER SECOND

Purpose: To compute meters per second(m/s) from miles per hour (mph).
Variables needed: M (mph).
Variables altered: None.
Variables returned: N (m/s).
Equations: m/s equals 0.447 mph
Source:

```
5 REM M/S
10 LET N=0.477*M
20 RETURN
```

Test Run For Meters Per Second (Miles)

```
RUN
INPUT VARIABLES:
?1
?2
```

50

```
?4
?8
?16
?32
?64
?128
?256
?512
RESULTS:
OUTPUT
INPUT    OUTPUT
1        0.4770000
2        0.9540000
4        1.9080000
8        3.8160000
16       7.6320000
32       15.264000
64       30.528000
128      61.056000
256      122.11200
512      244.22400
RUN COMPLETE
END*
```

MILES (STATUTE)

> **Purpose:** To compute miles (mi) from kilometers (km).
> **Variables needed:** K (km).
> **Variables altered:** None.
> **Variables returned:** M (mi)
> **Equations:** mi equals 0.6215 km
> **Source:**
> ```
> 5 REM MILES
> 10 LET M=0.6215*K
> 20 RETURN
> ```

Test Run For Miles (Statute)

```
RUN
INPUT VARIABLES:
?5
?10
?15
?20
?25
?30
?35
?40
?45
?50
?55
RESULTS:
OUTPUT
INPUT    OUTPUT
5        3.1075000
10       6.2150000
```

15	9.3225000
20	12.430000
25	15.537500
30	18.645000
35	21.752500
40	24.860000
45	27.967500
50	31.075000
55	34.182500

RUN COMPLETE
END*

MILES PER HOUR

Purpose: To compute miles per hour (mph) from meters per second (m/s).

Variables needed: M (m/s).

Variables altered: None.

Variables returned: N (mph).

Equations: mph equals 2.237 m/s

Source:
```
 5 REM MPH
10 LET N=2.237*M
20 RETURN
```

Test Run For Miles Per Hour

```
RUN
INPUT VARIABLES:
?1
?7
?49
?343
?2
?4
?8
?16
?3
?9
?27
RESULTS:
OUTPUT
```

INPUT	OUTPUT
1	2.2370000
7 ˙	15.659000
49	109.61300
343	767.29100
2	4.474000
4	8.9480000
8	17.896000
16	35.792000
3	6.7110000
9	20.133000
27	60.399000

RUN COMPLETE
END*

MILLILETER (CENTIMETER³)

Purpose: To compute milliliters (ml) from U.S. fluid ounces (oz)

Variables needed: Z (oz).

Variables altered: None.

Variables returned: M (ml).

Equations: ml equals 29.57 oz

Source:

```
5 REM ML (CM↑3)
10 LET M=29.57*Z
20 RETURN
```

Test Run For Milliliter

```
RUN
INPUT VARIABLES:
?1
?2
?3
?4
?5
?6
?7
?8
?9
?10
?11
RESULTS:
OUTPUT
INPUT    OUTPUT
1        29.570000
2        59.140000
3        88.710000
4        118.28000
5        147.85000
6        177.42000
7        206.99000
8        236.56000
9        266.13000
10       295.70000
11       325.27000
RUN COMPLETE
END*
```

MILLIMETERS

Purpose: To compute millimeters (mm) from inches (in).

Variables needed: I (in).

Variables altered: None.

Variables returned: M (mm).

Equations: mm equals 25.4 in

Source:

```
5 REM MILLIMETERS
10 LET M=25.4*I
20 RETURN
```

Test Run For Millimeters

```
RUN
INPUT VARIABLES:
?39
?39.5
?29
?29.5
?1
?2
?3
?4
?5
?6
?12
RESULTS:
OUTPUT
```

INPUT	OUTPUT
39	990.60000
39.5	1003.3000
29	736.60000
29.5	749.30000
1	25.400000
2	50.800000
3	76.200000
4	101.60000
5	127.00000
6	152.40000
12	304.80000

```
RUN COMPLETE
END*
```

MILLIMETERS OF MERCURY

Purpose: To compute millimeters of mercury (mm Hg) from
PASCALS (Pa).

Variables needed: P (Pa).

Variables altered: None.

Variables returned: M (mm Hg).

Equations: mm Hg equals 7.5019×10^{-3} Pa

Source:

```
5 REM MILLIMETERS OF MERCURY
10 LET M=7.5019-03*P
20 RETURN
```

Test Run For Millimeters of Mercury

```
RUN
INPUT VARIABLES:
```

```
?1
?1000
?500
?125
?250
?375
?750
?450
?600
?1200
?2400
RESULTS:
OUTPUT
INPUT   OUTPUT
1       7.5019E-03
1000    7.5019000
500     3.7509500
125     0.9377375
250     1.8754750
375     2.8132125
750.    5.6264250
450     3.3758550
600     4.5011400
1200    9.0022800
2400    18.004560
RUN COMPLETE
END*
```

NANOMETERS

Purpose: To compute nanometers (nm) from angstrom units (Å).

Variables needed: A (Å).

Variables altered: None.

Variables returned: N (nm).

Equations: nm equals 0.1 Å

Source:
```
 5 REM NANOMETERS
10 LET N=0.1*A
20 RETURN
```

NAUTICAL MILES

Purpose: To compute nautical miles (nmi) from kilometers (km).

Variables needed: K (km).

Variables altered: None.

Variables returned: N (nmi).

Equations: nmi equals 0.53996 km

Source:
```
 5 REM NAUTICAL MILES
10 LET N=0.53996*K
20 RETURN
```

Test Run For Nautical Miles

```
RUN
INPUT VARIABLES:
?1
?10
?20
?30
?40
?80
?160
?320
?640
?3
?9
RESULTS:
OUTPUT
```

INPUT	OUTPUT
1	0.5399600
10	5.3996000
20	10.799200
30	16.198800
40	21.598400
80	43.196800
160	86.393600
320	172.78720
640	345.57440
3	1.6198800
9	4.8596400

```
RUN COMPLETE
END*
```

NEWTONS

Purpose: To compute newtons (N) from ounce-force (oz).
Variables needed: Z (oz)
Variables altered: None.
Variables returned: N(N)
Equations: N equals 0.278 oz
Source:

```
 5 REM NEWTONS
10 LET N=0.278*Z
20 RETURN
```

Test Run For Newtons (Oz)

```
RUN
INPUT VARIABLES:
?9.81
?01
?4
?16
?64
?81
?27
```

56

```
?9
?3
?2
?1.5
RESULTS:
OUTPUT
INPUT   OUTPUT
9.81    2.7271800
1       0.2780000
4       1.1120000
16      4.4480000
64      17.792000
81      22.518000
27      7.5060000
9       2.5020000
3       0.8340000
2       0.5560000
1.5     0.4290000
RUN COMPLETE
END*
```

NEWTONS

Purpose: To compute newtons (N) from kilogram-force (Kg).
Variables needed: K (Kg).
Variables altered: None.
Variables returned: N (N).
Equations: N equals 9.807 Kg
Source:

```
 5 REM NEWTONS
10 LET N=9.807 K
20 RETURN
```

Test Run For Newtons Per Kilogram

```
RUN
INPUT VARIABLES:
?0.102
?1
?2
?4
?8
?16
?32
?9
?3
?27
?17
RESULTS:
OUTPUT
INPUT   OUTPUT
0.102   1.0003140
1       9.8070000
2       19.614000
```

4	39.228000
8	78.456000
16	156.91200
32	313.82400
9	88.263000
3	29.421000
27	264.78900
17	166.71900

RUN COMPLETE
END*

OUNCES

Purpose: To compute ounces (oz avdp-ounces) from grams (gm).

Variables needed: G (grams).

Variables altered: None.

Variables returned: Z (ounces).

Equations: oz equal 3.527×10^{-2} gm

Source:

```
 5 REM OUNCES
10 LET Z=3.527E-02*G
20 RETURN
```

Test Run For Ounces

RUN
INPUT VARIABLES:
?1
?28
?30
?32
?16
?8
?4
?3
?9
?27
?81
RESULTS:
OUTPUT

INPUT	OUTPUT
1	3.527E-02
28	0.98756000
30	1.05810000
32	1.12864000
16	0.56432000
8	0.28216000
4	0.14108000
3	0.10581000
9	0.31743000
27	0.95229000
81	2.85687000

RUN COMPLETE
END*

OUNCE FORCE

Purpose: To compute ounce-force (oz) from newtons (N).
Variables needed: N (N).
Variables altered: None.
Variables returned: Z (oz).
Equations: oz equal 3.597 N
Source:

```
5 REM OUNCES-FORCE
10 LET Z=3.597*N
20 RETURN
```

Test Run Ounce Force

```
RUN
INPUT VARIABLES:
?1
?2
?3
?4
?5
?6
?7
?8
?9
?18
?36
RESULTS:
OUTPUT
```

INPUT	OUTPUT
1	3.5970000
2	7.1940000
3	10.791000
4	14.388000
5	17.985000
6	21.582000
7	25.179000
8	28.776000
9	32.373000
18	64.746000
36	129.49200

```
RUN COMPLETE
END*
```

PASCALS

Purpose: To compute PASCALS (Pa) from millimeters of mercury (mm Hg).
Variables needed: M (mm Hz).
Variables altered: None.
Variables returned: P (Pa).
Equations: Pa equals 133.3 mm Hz
Source:

```
5 REM PASCALS
10 LET P=133.3*M
20 RETURN
```

Test Run For Pascals/Millimeters

```
RUN
INPUT VARIABLES:
?300
?290
?280
?310
?320
?107
?110
?55
?12
?17
RESULTS:
OUTPUT
```

INPUT	OUTPUT
300	39990.000
290	38657.000
280	37324.000
310	41323.000
320	42656.000
107	14263.100
110	14663.000
55	7331.5000
12	1599.6000
17	2266.1000

```
RUN COMPLETE
END*
```

PASCALS

Purpose: To compute Pascals from millibars (mb).
Variables needed: M (mb).
Variables altered: None.
Variables returned: P (Pascals).
Equations: Pa equals 100 mb
Source:

```
5 REM PASCALS
10 LET P=100*M
20 RETURN
```

Test Run For Pascals/Millibars

```
RUN
INPUT VARIABLES
?1
?2
?3
?4
?5
?64
```

```
?17
?33
?41
?97
?112
RESULTS:
OUTPUT
INPUT   OUTPUT
1       100
2       200
3       300
4       400
5       500
64      6400
17      1700
33      3300
41      4100
97      9700
112     11200
RUN COMPLETE
END*
```

PASCALS

Purpose: To compute Pascals from kilograms per square meter (Kg/M^2).

Variables needed: K (Kg/m^2).

Variables altered: None.

Variables returned: P (Pascals).

Equations: P equals 9.807 Kg/m^2

Source:

```
 5 REM PASCALS
10 LET P=9.807*K
20 RETURN
```

Test Run For Pascals/Kilograms

```
RUN
INPUT VARIABLES:
?0.102
?1
?2
?4
?8
?16
?32
?9
?3
?27
RESULTS:
OUTPUT
INPUT   OUTPUT
0.102   1.0003140
1       9.8070000
2       19.614000
```

```
4        39.228000
8        78.456000
16       156.91200
32       313.82400
9        88.263000
3        29.421000
27       264.78900
RUN COMPLETE
END*
```

PASCALS (Pa)

Purpose: To compute Pascals from pounds per foot^2 (lb/ft^2).
Variables needed: P (lb/ft^2).
Variables altered: None.
Variables returned: X (Pa).
Equations: Pa equals 47.88 lb/ft^2
Source:

```
 5 REM PASCALS
10 LET X=47.88*X
20 RETURN
```

Test Run For Pascals/LB

```
RUN
INPUT VARIABLES:
?1
?11
?22
?44
?88
?176
?352
?704
?1408
?2816
RESULTS:
OUTPUT
INPUT    OUTPUT
1        47.880000
11       526.68000
22       1053.3600
44       2106.7200
88       4213.4400
176      8426.8800
352      16853.760
704      33707.520
1408     67415.040
2816     134830.08
RUN COMPLETE
END*
```

POUNDS

Purpose: To compute pounds (lbs) from kilograms (Kg).
Variables needed: K (kilograms).

Variables altered: None.
Variables returned: P (pounds).
Equations: lb equals 2.2046 Kg
Source:

```
5 REM POUNDS
10 LET P=2.2046*K
20 RETURN
```

Test Run For Pounds

```
RUN
INPUT VARIABLES:
?1
?2
?5
?10
?15
?250
?500
?1000
?7
?11
?13
RESULTS:
OUTPUT
INPUT    OUTPUT
1        2.2046000
2        4.4092000
5        11.023000
10       22.046000
15       33.069000
250      551.15000
500      1102.3000
1000     2204.6000
7        15.432200
11       24.250600
13       28.659800
RUN COMPLETE
END*
```

POUND-FORCE

Purpose: To compute pound-force (lb) from newtons (N).
Variables needed: N (N).
Variables altered: None.
Variables returned: P (lb).
Equations: lb equals 0.2248 N
Source:

```
5 REM POUNDS-FORCE
10 LET P=0.2248*N
20 RETURN
```

Test Run For Pound-Force

```
RUN
INPUT VARIABLES:
?1
?4
?16
?64
?256
?2
?8
?32
?128
?3
?9
RESULTS:
OUTPUT
```

INPUT	OUTPUT
1	0.2248000
4	0.8992000
16	3.5968000
64	14.387200
256	57.548800
2	0.4496000
8	1.7984000
32	7.1936000
128	28.774400
3	0.674400
9	2.0232000

```
RUN COMPLETE
END*
```

POUNDS PER CUBIC FOOT

Purpose: To compute pounds per cubic foot (lb/ft^3) from kilograms per cubic meter (Kg/m^3).

Variables needed: K (Kg/m^3).

Variables altered: None.

Variables returned: P (lb/FT^3).

Equations: lb/ft^3 equals 6.242×10^{-2} Kg/m^3

Source:

```
5 REM POUNDS PER CUBIC FOOT
10 LET P=6.242 E-02*K
20 RETURN
```

Test Run For Pounds Per Cubic Foot

```
RUN
INPUT VARIABLES:
?1
?2
?4
?8
?16
?32
?64
```

```
?128
?256
?512
?2048
RESULTS:
OUTPUT
```

INPUT	OUTPUT
1	6.242E-02
2	0.1248400
4	0.2496800
8	0.4993600
16	0.9987200
32	1.9974400
64	3.9948800
128	7.9897600
256	15.979520
512	31.959040
2048	127.83616

```
RUN COMPLETE
END*
```

POUNDS PER SQUARE FOOT (lb/ft²)

Purpose: To compute pounds per square foot from Pascals.
Variables needed: P (pascal)
Variables altered: None.
Variables returned: L (lb/ft²)
Equations: lb/ft^2 equals 2.089×10^{-2} Pa
Source:

```
5 REM POUNDS PER SQUARE FOOT
10 LET L=2.089E-02*P
20 RETURN
```

Test Run For Pounds Per Square Foot

```
RUN
INPUT VARIABLES:
?100000
?101000
?50
?25
?75
?1
?200
?500
?30
?21
RESULTS:
OUTPUT
```

INPUT	OUTPUT
100000	2089.0000
101000	2109.8900
50	1.0445000
25	0.5222500
75	1.5667500

```
1          2.089E-02
200        4.1780000
500        10.445000
30         0.6267000
21         0.4386900
RUN COMPLETE
END*
```

POUNDS PER SQUARE INCH (lb/in²)

Purpose: To compute lb/in² from kPa (kiloPascals).
Variables needed: K (kPa).
Variables altered: None.
Variables returned: P (lb/in²).
Equations: lb/in² equals 0.14503 kPa
Source:

```
 5 REM POUNDS PER SQUARE INCH
10 LET P=0.14503*K
20 RETURN
```

Test Run For Pounds Per Square Inch

```
RUN
INPUT VARIABLES:
?1
?3
?9
?27
?81
?243
?256
?128
?64
?32
?16
RESULTS:
OUTPUT
INPUT   OUTPUT
1       0.1450300
3       0.4350900
9       1.3052700
27      3.9158100
81      11.747430
243     35.242290
256     37.127680
128     18.563840
64      9.2819200
32      4.6409600
16      2.3204800
RUN COMPLETE
END*
```

SQUARE CENTIMETERS

Purpose: To compute square centimeters (cm²) from square inches (in²).

Variables needed: I (in^2).
Variables altered: None.
Variables returned: C (cm^2).
Equations: cm^2 equals 6.452 in^2
Source:

```
5 REM SQ CENTIMETERS
10 LET C=452*I
20 RETURN
```

Test Run For Sq Centimeters

```
RUN
INPUT VARIABLES:
?1
?4
?9
?16
?25
?36
?49
?64
?81
?121
?144
RESULTS:
OUTPUT
```

INPUT	OUTPUT
1	6.4520000
4	25.808000
9	41.628304
16	103.23200
25	161.30000
36	232.27200
49	316.14800
64	412.92800
81	522.61200
121	780.69200
144	929.08800

```
RUN COMPLETE
END*
```

SQUARE FEET

Purpose: To compute square feet (ft^2) from square meters (m^2).
Variables needed: M (m^2).
Variables altered:81 None.
Variables returned: F (ft^2).
Equations: ft^2 equals 10.76426 m^2
Source:

```
5 REM SQ FEET
10 LET F=10.76426*M
20 RETURN
```

Test Run For Sq Feet

```
RUN
INPUT VARIABLES:
?1
?9
?640
?320
?160
?80
?40
?20
?18
?36
?72
?144
RESULTS:
OUTPUT
INPUT    OUTPUT
1        10.764260
9        96.878340
640      6889.1264
320      344.5632
160      1722.2816
80       861.14080
40       430.57040
20       215.28520
18       193.75668
36       387.51336
72       775.02672
144      1550.0534
RUN COMPLETE
END*
```

SQUARE MILES

Purpose: To compute square miles (mi^2) statute from square kilometers (km^2).

Variables needed: K (km^2).

Variables altered: None.

Variables returned: M (mi^2).

Equations: mi^2 equals 0.3861 km^2

Source:

```
 5 REM SQ MILES
10 LET M=0.3861*K
20 RETURN
```

Test Run For Square Miles

```
RUN
INPUT VARIABLES:
?1
?2
?4
?8
?16
?32
```

```
?64
?128
?256
?1024
?2048
RESULTS:
OUTPUT
INPUT    OUTPUT
1        0.3861000
2        0.7722000
4        1.5444000
8        3.0888000
16       6.1776000
32       12.355200
64       24.710400
128      49.420800
256      98.841600
1024     395.36640
2048     790.73280
RUN COMPLETE
END*
```

SQUARE YARDS

Purpose: To compute square yards (yd^2) from square meters (m^2).

Variables needed: M (m^2).

Variables altered: None.

Variables returned: Y (yd^2)

Equations: yd^2 equals 1.196029 m^2

Source:

```
5 REM SQ YARDS
10 LET Y=1.96029*M
20 RETURN
```

Test Run For Square Yards

```
RUN
INPUT VARIABLES:
?1
?3
?6
?9
?12
?15
?18
?21
?24
?27
?30
RESULTS:
OUTPUT
1        1.1960290
3        3.5880870
6        7.1761740
```

69

```
9       10.764261
12      14.352348
15      17.940435
18      21.528522
21      25.116609
24      28.704696
27      32.292783
30      35.880870
INPUT   OUTPUT
RUN COMPLETE
END*
```

WATTS

Purpose: To compute watts from BTU/Hr
Variables needed: B(BTU/Hr)
Variables altered: None.
Variables returned: W (watts)
Equations: watts equal 0.2931 BTU/Hr
Source:

```
5 REM WATTS
10 LET W=0.2931*B
20 RETURN
```

Test Run For Watts/BTU

```
RUN
INPUT VARIABLES:
?1
?2
?3
?4
?5
?6
?7
?8
?9
?10
?11
RESULTS:
OUTPUT
INPUT   OUTPUT
1       0.2931000
2       0.5862000
3       0.8793000
4       1.1724000
5       1.4655000
6       1.7586000
7       2.0517000
8       2.3448000
9       2.6379000
10      2.9310000
11      3.2241000

RUN COMPLETE
END*
```

WATTS (ELECTRICAL)

Purpose: To compute the number of watts produced by X horsepower (electric).
Variables needed: H (HP-horse-power).
Variables altered: None.
Variables returned: W (watts).
Equation: watts equal 746 HP
Source:

```
5 REM WATTS
10 LET W= 746*H
20 RETURN
```

Test Run For Watts/Hp

```
RUN
INPUT VARIABLES:
?0.25
?0.5
?0.75
?1
?2
?4
?5
?10
?20
?30
RESULTS:
OUTPUT
INPUT   OUTPUT
0.25    186.50000
0.5     373.00000
0.75    559.50000
1       746.00000
2       1492.0000
3       2238.0000
4       2984.0000
5       3730.0000
10      7460.0000
20      14920.000
30      22380.000
RUN COMPLETE
END*
```

YARDS

Purpose: To compute yards (yd) from meters (m).
Variables needed: M (m).
Variables altered: None.
Variables returned: Y (yd)
Equations: yd equals 1.0936 m
Source:

```
      5 REM YARDS
     10 LET Y=1.0936*M
     20 RETURN
```

Test Run For Yards

```
RUN
INPUT VARIABLES:
?1
?1.25
?2
?2.5
?3
?4
?5
?6
?7
?8
?9
RESULTS:
OUTPUT
INPUT   OUTPUT
1       1.0936000
1.25    1.3670000
2       2.1872000
2.5     2.7340000
3       3.2808000
4       4.3744000
5       5.4680000
6       6.5616000
7       7.6552000
8       8.7488000
9       9.8424000
RUN COMPLETE
END*
```

Chapter 4
Degrees, Grads and Radians

The three methods of measuring angles are:

—Degrees that divide a circle into four 90-unit sections (Fig. 4-1A).

—Grads that divide the circle in four 100-unit sections and are the *metric* replacement for degrees used in some parts of the world Fig. 4-1B).

—Radians that divide a circle into sections where the length of the arc of the section is equal to the radius of the circle (Fig. 4-1C). An arc is just a piece of the circumference.

Radians are the most "mathematical" of the angular types and are used by the computer. People usually prefer degrees and grads.

DEGREES TO RADIANS

Purpose: To convert degrees to radians.
Variables needed: D (degrees).
Variables altered: None.
Variables returned: R (radians).
Equations: $R=\pi D/180$
Source:

```
 5 REM DEGREES TO RADIANS
10 LET R=3.14159*D/180
20 RETURN
```

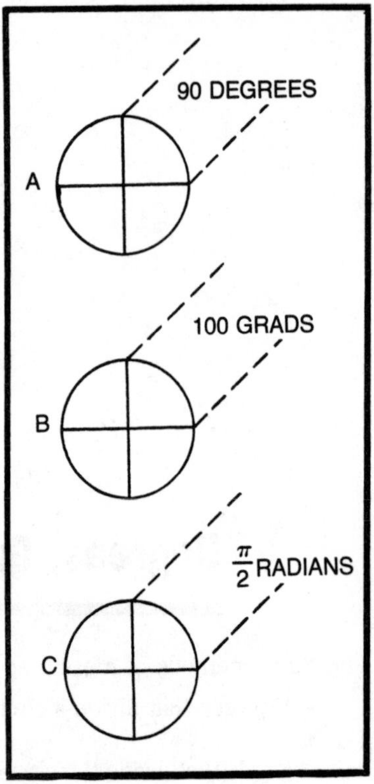

Fig. 4-1. Here are three ways to determine angles. A is degrees, B is grads and C is radians.

Test Run For Degrees To Radians

```
RUN
INPUT VARIABLES:
?1
?15
?30
?45
?69
?90
?105
?120
?135
?150
?165
RESULTS:
OUTPUT
INPUT    OUTPUT
1        1.745328E-02
15       0.2617991
30       0.5235983
45       0.7853975
60       1.0471967
90       1.5707950
105      1.8325940
```

120	2.0943930
135	2.3561925
150	2.6179917
165	2.8797910

RUN COMPLETE
END*

DEGREES TO GRADS

Purpose: To convert degrees to grads.
Variables needed: D (degrees).
Variables altered: None.
Variables returned: G (grads).
Equations: $G=10D/9$
Source:

```
 5 REM DEGREES TO GRADS
10 LET G=10*D/9
20 RETURN
```

Test Run For Degrees To Grads

RUN
INPUT VARIABLES:
?1
?15
?39
?45
?60
?90
?105
?120
?135
?150
RESULTS:
OUTPUT

INPUT	OUTPUT
1	1.1111111
15	16.666667
30	33.333333
45	50.000000
60	66.666667
90	100.00000
105	116.66667
120	133.33333
135	150.00000
150	166.66667

RUN COMPLETE
END*

GRADS TO DEGREES

Purpose: To convert grads to degrees.
Variables needed: G (grads).
Variables altered: None.
Variables returned: D (degrees).

Equations: $D = 9G/10$

Source:

```
5 REM GRADS TO DEGREES
10 LETD=9*G/10
20 RETURN
```

Test Run For Grads To Degrees

```
RUN
INPUT VARIABLES:
?1
?10
?20
?30
?40
?50
?60
?70
?80
?90
?100
RESULTS:
OUTPUT
```

INPUT	OUTPUT
1	0.9000000
10	9.0000000
20	18.000000
30	27.000000
40	36.000000
50	45.000000
60	54.000000
70	63.000000
80	72.000000
90	81.000000
100	90.000000

```
RUN COMPLETE
END*
```

GRADS TO RADIANS

Purpose: To convert grads to radians.
Variables needed: G (grads).
Variables altered: None.
Variables returned: R (radians).
Equations: $R = G/63.661977$
Source:

```
5 REM GRADS TO RADIANS
10 LET R=G/63.661977
20 RETURN
```

Test Run For Grads To Radians

```
RUN
INPUT VARIABLES:
?1
?10
```

```
?20
?30
?40
?50
?60
?70
?80
?90
?100
RESULTS:
OUTPUT
INPUT   OUTPUT
1       1.570796E-02
10      0.1570796
20      0.3141592
30      0.4712389
40      0.6283185
50      0.7853981
60      0.9424778
70      1.0995574
80      1.2566371
90      1.4137167
100     1.5707960
RUN COMPLETE
END*
```

RADIANS TO DEGREES

Purpose: To convert radians to degrees.

Variables needed: R (radians).

Variables altered: None.

Variables returned: D (degrees).

Equations: $D = 180R/\pi$

Source:
```
 5 REM RADIANS TO DEGREES
10 LET D=R*180/3.14159
20 RETURN
```

Test Run For Radians To Degrees

```
RUN
INPUT VARIABLES:
?0
?.1
?.2
?.3
?.4
?.5
?1
?2
?3
?4
?5
RESULTS:
OUTPUT
INPUT   OUTPUT
0       0.0000000
```

.1	5.7295828
.2	11.459160
.3	17.188748
.4	22.918312
.5	28.647914
1	57.295828
2	114.59166
3	171.88748
4	229.18312
5	286.47914

RUN COMPLETE
END*

RADIANS TO GRADS

Purpose: To convert radians to grads.
Variables needed: R (radians).
Variables altered: None.
Variables returned: G (grads).
Equation: $G = 63.661977R$
Source:

```
 5 REM RADIANS TO GRADS
10 LET G=63.661977*R
20 RETURN
```

Test Run For Radians To Grads

RUN
INPUT VARIABLES:
?0
?.1
?.2
?.3
?.4
?.5
?1
?2
?3
?4
?5
RESULTS:
OUTPUT

INPUT	OUTPUT
0	0.0000000
.1	6.3661977
.2	12.732395
.3	19.098593
.4	25.464791
.5	31.830989
1	63.661977
2	127.32395
3	190.98593
4	254.64791
5	318.30989

RUN COMPLETE
END*

78

Chapter 5
Electronics

The programs in this chapter will help you in common electronics problems.

CAPACITIVE TIME CONSTANT

Purpose: To find the capacitive time constant of a capacitor-resistor circuit.

Variables needed: C (capacitance in farads). R (resistance in ohms).

Variables altered: None.

Variables returned: T (capacitive time constant in seconds).

Equation: t=CR

Source:

```
 5 REM CAPACITIVE TIME CONSTANT
10 LET T=C*R
20 RETURN
```

Test Run For Capacitive Time Constant

```
RUN
INPUT VARIABLES:
?2.2E-06,2.2E07
?1E-07,1E05
?.2E-06,1E03
?2.0E-03,2E04
?3.3E-02,1E03
RESULTS:
OUTPUT
48.400000
0.0100000
0.0020000
40.000000
33.000000
RUN COMPLETE
END*
```

CURRENT POWER DISSIPATION

Purpose: To compute the power dissipation when current is known.

Variables needed: I (current in amperes). R (resistance in ohms).

Variables altered: None.

Variables returned: W (watts).

Equations: $W = I^2 R$

Source:

```
5 REM DISSIPATION (CURRENT)
10 LET W=I*I*R
20 RETURN
```

Test Run For Current Power

```
RUN
INPUT VARIABLES:
1,1
1,2
1,3
1,4
1,5
2,6
2,7
2,8
2,9
3,10
3,11
RESULTS OF SUBROUTINE:
OUTPUT
1.0000000
2.0000000
3.0000000
4.0000000
5.0000000
24.000000
28.000000
32.000000
36.000000
90.000000
99.000000
RUN TERMINATED
END*
```

INDUCTANCE

Purpose: To compute the inductance knowing the reactance and the frequency.

Variables needed: X (reactance in ohms). F (frequency in hertz).

Variables altered: None.

Variables returned: L (inductance in henries).
Equations: $L = X_L / 2\pi F$
Source:
```
 5 REM INDUCTANCE
10 LET L=X/(2*3.14159*F)
20 RETURN
```

Test Run For Inductance

```
RUN
INPUT VARIABLES:
?1,1000
?2,2000
?3,2000
?4,2000
?5,2000
?6,1000
?7,1000
?8,1000
?9,3000
?10,3000
?11,3000
RESULT:
OUTPUT
```

INPUT	OUTPUT
1,1000	1.59E-04
2,2000	1.59E-04
3,2000	2.38E-04
4,2000	3.18E-04
5,2000	3.97E-04
6,1000	9.54E-04
7,1000	1.11E-03
8,1000	1.27E-02
9,3000	4.77E-04
10,3000	5.30E-04
11,3000	5.83E-04

```
RUN COMPLETE
END*
```

INDUCTIVE TIME CONSTANT

Purpose: To find the time constant of an inductor-resistor circuit.

Variables needed: L (Henries). R (ohms).

Variables altered: None.

Variables returned: T (time constant in seconds).

Equations: $t = \dfrac{L}{R}$

Source:
```
 5 REM INDUCTIVE TIME CONSTANT
10 LET T=L/R
20 RETURN
```

Test Run For Inductive Time Constant

```
RUN
INPUT VARIABLES:
?.01,1000
?.1,1000
?.2,1000
?.01,2000
?.02,2000
?.3,2000
?.01,5000
?.1,5000
?.2,5000
?.3,5000
?.7,9000
RESULTS:
OUTPUT
INPUT        OUTPUT
?01,1000     1.0E-05
?.1,1000     1.0E-04
?.2,1000     2.0E-04
?.01,2000    5.0E-06
?.02,2000    1.0E-04
?.3,2000     1.5E-04
?.01,5000    2.0E-06
?.1,5000     2.0E-05
?.2,5000     4.0E-05
?.3,5000     6.0E-05
?.7,9000     7.78E-05

RUN COMPLETE
END*
```

JOULE'S LAW

Purpose: To compute the energy or calories (cal) expended in one (1) second by a current of one (1) ampere at a potential of one (1) volt.

Variables needed: I (amperes). T (time in seconds). R (resistance in ohms).

Variables altered: None.

Variables returned: C (calories/energy).

Equations: $C=(I^2RT)/4.19$

Source:

```
5 REM JOULE'S LAW
10 LET C=(I*I*R*T)/4.19
20 RETURN
```

Test Run For Joules Law

```
RUN
INPUT VARIABLES:
1,2,3
4,5,6
```

```
7,8,9
10,11,12
13,14,15
16,17,18
1,4,7
2,5,8
3,6,9
1,5,9
3,5,7
RESULTS OF SUBROUTINE:
OUTPUT
1.4319809
114.55847
842.00477
3150.3580
8470.1671
18695.943
6.6825776
38.186158
115.99045
10.739857
75.178998
RUN TERMINATED
END*
```

OHM'S LAW

OHM'S LAW simply states that current is proportional to voltage, when the voltage is constant. Constant equates with steady state. That is: E kI

The value k is equal to E/I and is called the resistance. The measure of E (also known as the electromotive force) is voltage. This law is the basic foundation for all electronic circuits. These subroutines show how to calculate any value, given the other two.

OHM'S LAW (CURRENT)

Purpose: To find the current when the voltage and resistance is known.

Variables needed: E (voltage in volts). R (resistance in ohms).

Variables altered: None.

Variables returned: I (current in amperes).

Equations: $I = E/R$

Source:

```
 5 REM OHMS LAW (CURRENT)
10 LET I=E/R
20 RETURN
```

Test Run For Ohm's Law (Current)

```
RUN
INPUT VARIABLES:
1,1
```

```
1,2
1,3
1,4
1,5
2,6
2,7
2,8
2,9
2,10
3,11
RESULTS OF SUBROUTINE:
OUTPUT
1.0000000
0.5000000
0.3333333
0.2500000
0.2000000
0.3333333
0.2857143
0.2500000
0.2222222
0.1000000
0.2727273
RUN TERMINATED
END*
```

OHM'S LAW (RESISTANCE)

Purpose: To compute the resistance when the current and the voltage are known.

Variables needed: I (current in amperes). E (voltage in volts).

Variables altered: None.

Variables returned: R (resistance in ohms).

Equations: $R = E/I$

Source:
```
 5 REM OHMS LAW (RESISTANCE)
10 LET R=E/I
20 RETURN
```

Test Run For Ohms Law (Resistance)
```
RUN
INPUT VARIABLES
1,1
2,1
3,1
4,1
5,1
6,2
7,2
8,2
9,2
10,2
11,3
```

RESULTS OF SUBROUTINE:
OUTPUT
1.0000000
2.0000000
3.0000000
4.0000000
5.0000000
3.0000000
3.5000000
4.0000000
4.5000000
5.0000000
3.6666667
RUN TERMINATED
END*

OHM'S LAW (VOLTAGE)

Purpose: To compute the voltage when the current and the resistance is known.

Variables needed: I (current in amperes). R (resistance in ohms).

Variables altered: None.

Variables returned: E (voltage in volts).

Equations: E=IR

Source:
```
 5 REM OHMS LAW (VOLTAGE)
10 LET E=I*R
20 RETURN
```

Test Run For Ohms Law (Voltage)

RUN
INPUT VARIABLES:
1,11
1,10
1,9
1,8
1,7
2,6
2,5
2,4
2,3
3,1
RESULTS OF SUBROUTINE:
OUTPUT
11.000000
10.000000
9.0000000
8.0000000
7.0000000
12.000000
10.000000
8.0000000
6.0000000

3.0000000
RUN TERMINATED
END*

PARALLEL RESISTANCE

Purpose: To compute the total parallel resistance of a circuit with two resistors in parallel.

Variables needed: R1 (1st resistance in ohms). R2 (2nd resistance in ohms).

Variables altered: None.

Variables returned: T (total parallel resistance of the two resistors).

Equation: $R_p = R_1R_2/R_1 + R_2$

Source:

```
 5 REM PARALLEL RESISTANCE
10 LET T = (R1*R2)/(R1 + R2)
20 RETURN
```

Test Run For Parallel Resistance

```
RUN
INPUT VARIABLES:
1,1
1,2
1,3
1,4
1,5
2,6
2,7
2,8
2,9
3,10
3,11
RESULTS OF SUBROUTINE:
OUTPUT
0.5000000
0.6000000
0.7500000
0.800000
0.8333333
1.5000000
1.5555555
1.6000000
1.6363636
2.3076923
2.3571429
RUN TERMINATED
END*
```

SERIES CAPACITANCE

Purpose: To compute the series capacitance of two capacitors in series.

Variables needed: C1 (1st capacitance in MFD). C2 (2nd capacitance in MFD).

Variables altered: None.

Variables returned: T (total series capacitance of two capacitors in series).

Equations: $C_s = C_1 C_2 / C_1 + C_2$

Source:

```
 5 REM SERIES CAPACITANCE
10 LET T=(C1*C2)/(C1+C2)
20 RETURN
```

Test Run For Series Capacitance

```
RUN
INPUT VARIABLES:
1,1
2,2
3,3
4,4
5,5
1,6
2,7
3,8
4,9
5,10
RESULTS OF SUBROUTINE:
OUTPUT
0.5000000
1.0000000
1.5000000
2.0000000
2.5000000
0.8571429
1.5555556
2.1818182
2.7692308
3.3333333
4.2777778
RUN TERMINATED
END*
```

VOLTAGE POWER DISSIPATION

Purpose: To compute the power dissipation when current is known.

Variables needed: E (voltage in volts). R (resistance in ohms).

Variables altered: None.

Variables returned: W (power dissipation in watts)

Equations: $W = E^2 / R$

Source:

```
 5 REM DISSIPATION (VOLTAGE)
10 LET W=E*E/R
20 RETURN
```

Test Run For Voltage Power

```
RUN
INPUT VARIABLES:
1,1
2,1
3,1
4,1
5,1
6,2
7,2
8,2
9,2
10,3
11,4
RESULTS OF SUBROUTINE:
OUTPUT
1.0000000
4.0000000
9.0000000
16.000000
25.000000
18.000000
24.500000
32.000000
40.500000
33.333333
30.250000
RUN TERMINATED
END*
```

Graphs
Chapter 6

Purpose: To allow graphing of a series of positive values by generating the graph lines one at a time, including scaling.

This programming routine generates a line, but does not print it. The line is divided into 64 increments—available in most machines—but it can be changed if your version of BASIC or your terminal is set up differently. You can output the generated line with a comment or number if you have the room and wish to do so.

Variables needed: M (maximum value being plotted). V (value currently being plotted).

Variables altered: X (working value used to index into the string).

Variables returned: G$ (string—length 64 (DIM G$(64))—containing the generated line).

Source:
```
1 REM GENERATES A GRAPH-LINE FOR PRINTING
2 REM V IS THE INPUT VALUE
3 REM M IS THE MAXIMUM VALUE
4 REM G$ IS THE GRAPH-LINE
10 LET G$= " "
20 LET X=INT (V/M*64+0.5)
30 IF X>0 THEN 50
40 LET X=1
50 IF X<65 THEN 70
60 LET X=64
70 LET SUBSTR(G$, X, 1) = "*"
80 RETURN
```

Note: The reference to the DIM statement under the heading **Variables returned** applies to those versions of BASIC that require a string variable to be dimensioned with respect to character length as well as to the number of strings in a list or array.

CENTER-GRAPH

Purpose: This routine divides a graph into 32 positive and 32 negative points. It places a dot in the center (zero) and an asterisk in the same line proportionately located for the purposes of creating a visual representation of the value. Scaling is automatic, since the maximum value is also required.

Variables needed: M (maximum value of all lines processed—use maximum value *finder* if a table is being graphed). V (value to be graphed).

Variables altered: X (index to graph being generated).

Variables returned: G$ (string—length 64 (DIM G$(64))— containing the generated line of the graph).

Source:

```
1 REM CENTERS A VALUE IN
2 REM A GRAPH-LINE FOR PRINTING
3 REM M IS THE LARGEST VALUE (ABSOLUTE)
4 REM V IS THE INPUT VALUE
5 REM G$ IS THE GRAPH-LINE
10 LET G$= " "
20 LET SUBSTR(G$,32,1)= " . "
30 IF V<0 THEN 80
40 LET X=INT(V/M*32+32.5)
50 IF X<65 THEN 110
60 LET X=64
70 GOTO 110
80 LET X=INT(32-ABS(V/M)*32)
90 IF X>0 THEN 110
100 LET X=1
110 LET SUBSTR(G$, X, 1) = "*"
120 RETURN
```

Note: The reference to the DIM statement under the heading **Variables returned** applies to those versions of BASIC that require a string variable to be dimensioned with respect to character length as well as to the number of strings in a list or array.

HISTOGRAPHICS

Purpose: A histogram or *bar-chart* is a pictorial representation of a series of values in the form of *bars*. The routine shown generates a bar of asterisks of a length proportional to the input values. It further compensates for truncation errors (loss of digits) and scales the graph by using the largest value expected. If the values are already in a table, use maximum value *finder* to obtain the scaling factor.

Variables needed: M (maximum value to be output). V (value to be graphed).

Variables altered: X (range value giving size of bar). I (loop counter for inserting asterisks).

Variables returned: G$ (string—length 64 (DIM G$(64)) containing the bar).

Source:

```
1 REM GENERATES A HISTOGRAM GRAPH-LINE
2 REM M IS THE MAXIMUM VALUE
3 REM V IS THE INPUT VALUE
4 REM G$ IS THE GRAPH-LINE
10 LET G$= " "
20 LET X=INT(V/M*64+0.5)
30 IF X<65 THEN 50
40 LET X=64
50 FOR I=1 TO X
60 LET SUBSTR (G$,I,1)= " * "
70 NEXT I
80 RETURN
```

Note: The reference to the DIM statement under the heading **Variables returned** applies to those versions of BASIC that require a string variable to be dimensioned with respect to character length as well as to the number of strings in a list or array).

Test Run For Histographics

```
RUN
INPUT VARIABLES:
?64
?1
?2
?3
?4
?23
?7
?19
?1
?8
?19
RESULTS:
OUTPUT
INPUT    OUTPUT
1        *
2        **
3        ***
4        ****
23       ***********************
7        *******
19       *******************
1        *
8        ********
19       *******************
RUN COMPLETE
END*
```

Chapter 7
Hyperbolics

Hyperbolics are functions based on a hyperbola, just as the better known trigonometric functions are based on the circle. They are often used in electronics and physics.

HYPERBOLIC FUNCTIONS

Purpose: The following routines provide the hyperbolic functions:

SINH (X)	SINH^{-1}(X)
COSH(X)	COSH^{-1}(X)
TANH(X)	TANH^{-1}(X)
CSCH(X)	CSCH^{-1}(X)
SECH(X)	SECH^{-1}(X)
COTH(X)	COTH^{-1}(X)

Variables needed: X (argument of the hyperbolic function).
Variables altered: None.
Variables returned: Y (resultant value).
Equations:

$$\sinh(X) = \frac{e^x - e^{-x}}{2}$$

$$\cosh(X) = \frac{e^x + e^x}{2}$$

$$\tanh(X) = \frac{e^x - e^{-x}}{e^x + e^{-x}}$$

$csch(X) = 1/\sinh x$
$sech(X) = 1/\cosh x$
$coth(X) = 1/\tanh x$
$\sinh^{-1}(X)=Ln(X + (X^2 + 1)^{1/2})$
$\cosh^{-1}(X)=Ln(X + (X^2 - 1)^{1/2})$
$\tanh^{-1}(X)=\frac{1}{2}Ln(1 + X/1 - X)$
$csch^{-1}(X)=\sinh^{-1}(1/x)$
$sech^{-1}(X)=\cosh^{-1}(1/x)$
$coth^{-1}(X)=\tanh^{-1}(1/x)$

SINH(X)

```
 5 REM SINH
10 LET Y=(EXP (X)-EXP(-X))/2
20 RETURN
```

COSH(X)

```
 5 REM COSH
10 LET Y=(EXP(X)+EXP(-X))/2
20 RETURN
```

TANH(X)

```
 5 REM TANH
10 LET Y=(EXP (X)-EXP(-X))/(EXP (X)+EXP(-X))
20 RETURN
```

CSCH(X)

```
 5 REM CSCH
10 LET Y=1/((EXP (X)-EXP (-X))/2)
20 RETURN
```

SECH(X)

```
 5 REM SECH
10 LET Y=1/((EXP (X)+EXP(-X))/2)
20 RETURN
```

COTH(X)

```
 5 REM COTH
10 LET Y=1/((EXP (X)-EXP (-X))/(EXP (X)+EXP (-X)))
20 RETURN
```

SINH$_{-1}$(X)

```
 5 REM SINH-1
10 LET Y=LOG(X+SQR(X*X+1))
20 RETURN
```

COSH⁻¹ (X)

```
 5 REM COSH-1
10 LET Y=LOG(X+SQR(X*X−1))
20 RETURN
```

TANH⁻¹ (X)

```
 5 REM TANH-1
10 LET Y=(LOG((1+X)/(1−X)))/2
20 RETURN
```

CSCH⁻¹ (X)

```
 5 REM CSCH−1
10 LET Y=LOG((1/x)+SQR((1/X)*(1/X)+1))
20 RETURN
```

SECH⁻¹ (X)

```
 5 REM SECH−1
10 LET Y=LOG((1/X)+SQR((1/X)*(1/X)−1))
20 RETURN
```

COTH⁻¹ (X)

```
 5 REM COTH−1
10 LET Y=(LOG((+(1/X))/(1−(1/X))))/2
20 RETURN
```

Test Run For SINH
```
RUN
INPUT VARIABLES:
?1
?2
?3
?4
?5
?6
?7
?8
?9
?10
RESULTS:
OUTPUT
INPUT   OUTPUT
1       1.1752012
2       3.6268604
```

94

3	10.017875
4	27.289917
5	74.203211
6	210.71316
7	548.31612
8	1490.4788
9	4051.5419
10	11013.233

RUN COMPLETE
END*

Test Run For COSH

RUN
INPUT VARIABLES:
?1
?2
?3
?4
?5
?6
?7
?8
?9
?10
RESULTS:
OUTPUT

INPUT	OUTPUT
1	1.5430806
2	3.7621957
3	10.067662
4	27.308233
5	74.209949
6	201.71564
7	548.31704
8	1490.4792
9	4051.5420
10	11013.233

RUN COMPLETE
END*

Test Run For TANH

RUN
INPUT VARIABLES;
?1
?2
?3
?4
?5
?6
?7
?8
?9
?10
RESULTS:
OUTPUT

INPUT	OUTPUT
1	0.7615942
2	0.9640276
3	0.9950548
4	0.9993293
5	0.9999092
6	0.9999877
7	0.9999983
8	0.9999997
9	1.0000000
10	1.0000000

RUN COMPLETE
END*

Test Run For CSCH

RUN
INPUT VARIABLES:
?0.1
?0.2
?0.3
?0.6
?0.7
?0.8
?0.9
?1
?0.4
RESULTS:
OUTPUT

INPUT	OUTPUT
.1	9.9833528
.2	4.9668216
.3	3.2838534
.6	1.5707129
.7	1.3182461
.8	1.1259917
.9	0.8509181
1	2.4345571
.4	1.1919034

RUN COMPLETE
END*

Test Run For SECH

RUN
INPUT VARIABLES:
?.1
?.2
?.3
?.4
?.5
?.6
?.7
?.8
?.9
?1

RESULTS:
OUTPUT
INPUT	OUTPUT
.1	0.9950207
.2	0.9803280
.3	0.9566279
.4	0.9250075
.5	0.8868189
.6	0.8435507
.7	0.7967055
.8	0.7476999
.9	0.6977946
1	0.6480543
RUN COMPLETE
END*

Test Run For ASINH

RUN
INPUT VARIABLES:
?1
?2
?3
?4
?5
?6
?7
?8
?9
?10
?11
RESULTS:
OUTPUT
INPUT	OUTPUT
1	0.8813736
2	1.4436355
3	1.8184465
4	2.0947125
5	2.3124383
6	2.4917799
7	2.6441208
8	2.7764723
9	2.8934400
10	2.9982230
11	3.0931022
RUN COMPLETE
END*

Test Run For ACOSH

RUN
INPUT VARIABLES:
?1
?2
?3
?4

?5
?6
?7
?8
?9
?10
?11
RESULTS:
OUTPUT

INPUT	OUTPUT
1.	0.0000000
2	1.3169579
3	1.7627472
4	2.0634371
5	2.2924317
6	2.4778887
7	2.6339158
8	2.7686594
9	2.8872710
10	2.9932228
11	3.0889699

RUN COMPLETE
END*

Test Run For ATANH

RUN
INPUT VARIABLES;
?0
?.1
?.2
?.3
?.4
?.5
?.6
?.7
?.8
?.9
?.95
RESULTS:
OUTPUT

INPUT	OUTPUT
0	0.0000000
.1	0.1003353
.2	0.2027326
.3	0.3095196
.4	0.4236489
.5	0.5493061
.6	0.6931472
.7	0.8673005
.8	1.0986123
.9	1.4722195
.95	1.8317808

RUN COMPLETE
END*

Test Run For ACSCH

```
RUN
INPUT VARIABLES:
?1
?2
?3
?4
?5
?6
?7
?8
?9
?10
?11
RESULTS:
OUTPUT
```

INPUT	OUTPUT
1	0.8813736
2	0.4812118
3	0.3274502
4	0.2474665
5	0.1986901
6	0.1659046
7	0.1423756
8	0.1246767
9	0.1108837
10	0.0998341
11	0.0907843

```
RUN COMPLETE
END*
```

Test Run For ASECH

```
RUN
INPUT VARIABLES:
?.1
?.2
?.3
?.4
?.5
?.6
?.7
?.8
?.9
?.95
?1
RESULTS:
OUTPUT
```

INPUT	OUTPUT
.1	2.9932228
.2	2.2924317
.3	1.8738202
.4	1.5667992
.5	1.3169579
.6	1.0986123

```
.7          0.8955881
.8          0.6931472
.9          0.4671453
.95         0.3230364
1           0.0000000
RUN COMPLETE
END*
```

Test Run For ACOTH

```
RUN
INPUT VARIABLES:
?1.1
?2
?3
?4
?5
?6
?7
?8
?9
?10
?11
RESULTS:
OUTPUT
INPUT   OUTPUT
1.1     1.5222612
2       0.5493061
3       0.3465736
4       0.2554128
5       0.2027326
6       0.1682361
7       0.1438410
8       0.1256572
9       0.1115718
10      0.1003353
11      0.0911608
RUN COMPLETE
END*
```

Chapter 8
Inertia

The moment of inertia of an object is the measure of how difficult it is to start an object turning or to stop it from turning once it is going. In terms of mechanics: $T=QI$ where T is the torque, Q is the angular acceleration and I is the amount of inertia.

Energy (as in a flywheel) can be given as: $E/W^2I/2$, where E is the energy and W is the spin rate (in radians per second).

If the spin is given in revolutions per second, then the formula becomes: $E=2\pi^2R^2I$ where R is the spin in revolutions per second.

Moments of inertia are particularly valuable in physics and for mechanics and mechanical engineers.

ANNULAR SECTION MOMENT OF INERTIA

Purpose: To compute the moment of inertia of an annular section (Fig. 2-7).

Variables needed: D1 (inside diameter of the annulus). D2 (outside diameter of the annulus).

Variables altered: None.

Variables returned: M (moment of inertia of the annulus).

Equations: $M(\pi(d_2^4-d_1^4))/64$

Source:
```
5 REM POLAR MOMENT OF INERTIA OF AN ANNULUS
10 LET M = (3.14159*(D2↑4-D1↑4))/164
20 RETURN
```

Test Run For Annular (Moment)

```
RUN
INPUT VARIABLES:
1,2
3,4
5,6
7,8
9,10
11,12
13,14
15,16
17,18
19,20
21,22
RESULTS OF SUBROUTINE:
OUTPUT
0.7363102
8.5902852
32.937608
83.203048
168.81138
299.18736
483.75577
731.94138
1053.1690
1456.8633
1952.4491
RUN TERMINATED
END*
```

ANNULAR SECTION POLAR MOMENT OF INERTIA

Purpose: To compute the polar moment of inertia of an annulus.

Variables needed: D1 (inside diameter of the annulus). D2 (outside diameter of the annulus).

Variables altered: None.

Variables returned: P (polar moment of inertia of the annulus).

Equations: $P = (\pi(D_2^4 - D_1^4))/32$

Source:

```
5 REM POLAR MOMENT OF INERTIA OF AN ANNULUS
10 LET P = (3.14159*(D2↑4-D1↑4))/32
20 RETURN
```

Test Run For Annular (Polar)

```
RUN
INPUT VARIABLES
1,2
3,4
5,6
7,8
9,10
```

```
11,12
13,14
15,16
17,18
19,20
21,22
```
RESULTS OF SUBROUTINE:
 OUTPUT
1.4726203
17.180570
65.875215
166.40610
337.62275
598.37472
967.51155
1463.8828
2106.3379
2913.7266
3904.8982
RUN TERMINATED
END*

CIRCULAR MOMENT OF INERTIA

Purpose: To compute the moment of inertia in a circle.

Variables needed: D (diameter of the circle).

Variables altered: None.

Variables returned: M (moment of inertia of the circle).

Equations: $M = \pi d^4/64$

Source:
```
 5 REM MOMENT OF INERTIA OF A CIRCLE
10 LET M=(3.14159*D↑4)/64
20 RETURN
```

Test Run For Circular (Moment)

RUN
INPUT VARIABLES:
```
1
2
3
4
5
6
7
8
9
10
11
```
 RESULTS OF SUBROUTINE:
 OUTPUT
4.909E-02
0.7853975
3.9760748
12.566360
30.679590

63.617198
117.85871
201.06176
322.06206
490.87344
718.68780
RUN TERMINATED
   END*

CIRCULAR POLAR MOMENT OF INERTIA

Purpose: To compute the polar moment of inertia of a circle.
Variables needed: D (diameter of the circle).
Variables altered: None.
Variables returned: P (polar moment of inertia).
Equations: $P = \pi d^4/32$
Source:

```
5 REM CIRCULAR POLAR MOMENT OF INERTIA
10 LET P = (3.14159*D ↑ 4)/32
20 RETURN
```

Test Run For Circular (Polar)

RUN
INPUT VARIABLES:
1
2
3
4
5
6
7
8
9
10
11
RESULTS OF SUBROUTINE:
OUTPUT
9.817E-02
1.5707950
7.9521497
25.132720
61.359180
127.23439
235.71742
402.12352
644.12412
981.74688
1437.3756
RUN TERMINATED
END*

104

RECTANGULAR MOMENT OF INERTIA

Purpose: To compute the moment of inertia of a rectangle.

Variables needed: B (length of base) H (length of height in same units as base).

Variables altered: None.

Variables returned: M (moment of inertia).

Equations: $M = bh^3/12$

Source:
```
 5 REM RECTANGULAR MOMENT OF INERTIA
10 LET M = (B*H*H*H)/12
20 RETURN
```

Test Run For Rectangular (Moment)
```
RUN
INPUT VARIABLES:
1,1
1,2
1,3
1,4
1,5
2,6
2,7
2,8
2,9
2,10
3,11
RESULTS OF SUBROUTINE:
OUTPUT
8.33E-02
0.6666667
2.2500000
5.3333333
10.416667`
36.000000
57.166667
85.333333
121.50000
166.66667
332.75000
RUN TERMINATED
END*
```

RECTANGULAR SECTION POLAR MOMENT OF INERTIA

Purpose: To compute the polar moment of inertia of a rectangular section.

Variables needed: B (base of rectangle). H (height of rectangle).

Variables altered: None.

Variables returned: P (polar moment of inertia of the rectangle).

105

Equations: $P = \dfrac{bh\,(b^2 + h^2)}{12}$

Source:
```
 5 REM POLAR MOMENT OF INERTIA OF A RECTANGLE
10 LET P = (B*H*(B*B+H*H))/12
20 RETURN
```

Test Run For Rectangular (Polar)

```
RUN
INPUT VARIABLES:
1,1
1,2
1,3
1,4
1,5
2,6
2,7
2,8
2,9
2,10
3,11
RESULTS OF SUBROUTINE:
OUTPUT
0.1666667
0.8333333
2.5000000
5.6666667
10.833333
40. 000000
61, 833333
90,666667
127.50000
173.33333
357.50000
RUN TERMINATED
END*
```

The programs in this chapter concern the operations and relationships of numbers.

ARC

Purpose: To compute the length of an arc of a circle (Fig. 2-2).

Variables needed: R (radius of circle). A (measure in degrees of its (arc) central angle).

Variables altered: None.

Variables returned: L (length).

Equations: L=RT where T is in radians.

Source:

```
 5 REM ARC
10 LET L=R*(A*3.14159/180)
20 RETURN
```

Test Run For Arc

```
RUN
INPUT VARIABLES:
?15,2
?30,2
?45,2
?60,2
?90,2
RESULTS:
OUTPUT
0.5235983
1.0471967
1.5707950
2.0943933
3.1415900
RUN COMPLETE
END*
```

AREA OF A CIRCLE

Purpose: To compute the area of a circle when the radius is known.

Variables needed: R (radius).

Variables altered: None.

Variables returned: A (area).

Equations: $a = \pi r^2$

Source:

```
5 REM AREA OF A CIRCLE
10 LET A=3.14159*R*R
20 RETURN
```

Test Run For Area Of A Circle

```
RUN
INPUT VARIABLES:
?1
?2
?3
?4
?5
RESULTS:
OUTPUT
3.1415900
12.566360
28.274310
50.265440
78.539750
RUN COMPLETE
END*
```

ARITHMETIC PROGRESSION

Purpose: To compute the arithmetic progression knowing the first term, the common difference and the number of terms.

Variables needed: A (the first term in the sequence). D (the common difference between terms). N (number of terms in the sequence).

Variables altered: I (counter in the FOR-NEXT loop).

Variables returned: J (sum of the series). K (the kth element of the series). L (the value of the kth element in the series).

Source:

```
5 REM ARITHMETIC PROGRESSION
10 J=0
20 FOR I=0 TO N-1
30 K=I+1
40 L=A+(I*D)
50 J=J+L
60 PRINT K,L
70 NEXT I
80 PRINT "SUM";J
90 RETURN
```

Note: Line 60 can be removed if you do not want that table to be printed. Line 80, which prints the sum, can also be removed.

Test Run For Arithmetic Progression

```
RUN
INPUT VARIABLES:
?10,2,5
RESULTS:
OUTPUT
TERM NUMBER     TERM PROGRESSION        SUM
1               10                      70
2               12
3               14
4               16
5               18
RUN COMPLETE
END*
```

BINARY SEARCH

Purpose: This routine searches a table that has either been sorted in ascending sequence or created in ascending sequence—see table sort—by successively halving the search area. This continuous division by two is called *binary searching*. Although more complex than a simple scan (see sequential search) the routine is capable of enormously higher speed on large tables. The search speed is proportional to:

$$INT(LOG_2N)+1$$

Variables needed: X (value being searched for). T (sorted table to be searched). N (size of sorted table).

Variables altered: M1 (low boundary of table section being searched). M2 (high boundary of table section being searched). M3 (location of current search point—calculated from M1 and M2).

Warning: If the table is not in sequence this routine might act unpredictably. For example, it might loop or give the wrong results.

Variables returned: L (location in the table of found value if not set to zero, no such value if set to zero).

Source:

```
 1 REM THIS ROUTINE SEARCHES A SORTED
 2 REM TABLE USING A BINARY-SEARCH
 3 REM TECHNIQUE
10 LET M1=1
20 LET M2=N
30 LET M3=INT((M1+M2+1)/2)
40 IF X=T(M3) THEN 130
50 IF M3=M2 OR M3=M1 THEN 110
60 IF X<T(M3) THEN 90
```

```
70 LET M1=M3
80 GOTO 30
90 LET M2=M3
100 GOTO 30
105 REM NOT FOUND, NOT IN TABLE
110 LET L=0
120 GOTO 140
130 LET L=M3
140 RETURN
```

Test Run For Binary Search

```
RUN
INPUT VARIABLES
?12
?1,3,5,8,11,12,15,24,25,26
?10
RESULTS:
OUTPUT
6
RUN COMPLETE
/CHANGE X,9
RUN
RESULTS
OUTPUT
0
RUN COMPLETE
END*
```

COMPLEX VARIABLES

Complex numbers contain a *real* part and an *imaginary* part and are usually written as: A+Bi A is the real part and the B is the imaginary component. The i stands for the square root of minus one. This format is called *Cartesian* representation.

An alternative representation is: $re^{i\theta}$ or $r(\cos\theta + i\sin\theta)$. This format is called polar form.

Complex numbers and complex functions are used in electronics, phyics and mathematics. Several computer languages (such as Fortran and APL) provide complex functions automatically. BASIC does not. This book gives you these functions for use in BASIC.

COMPLEX OPERATIONS

Purpose: To solve the following functions:
—complex add.
—complex subtraction.
—complex multiplication.
—complex division.
—complex reciprocal.
—complex absolute.

110

—complex square.
—complex square root.
—complex natural log.
—complex exponential.

Variables needed: A1 (real part of first complex number). B1 (imaginary part of first complex number). A2 (real part of second number if required). B2 (imaginary part of second number if required).

Variables altered: None.

Variables returned: A (real part). B (imaginary part). C (absolute value).

Equations:

Complex add: $(A_1+iB_1)+(A_2+iB_2)= (A_1+A_2)+i(B_1+B_2)$

Complex subtraction: $(A_1+iB_1)-(A_2+iB_2)= (A_1-A_2)+i(B_1-B_2)$

Complex multiplication: $(A_1+iB_1)(A_2+iB_2)= (A_1A_2-B_1B_2) +i(A_1B_2+A_2B_1)$

Complex division: $(A_1+iB_1) \} (A_2+iB_2) = (A_1A_2+B_1B_2)+i (A_2B_1-A_1B_2)/A_2^2 + B_2^2$

Complex reciprocal: $\dfrac{1}{A+iB} = \dfrac{A-iB}{A^2+B^2}$

Complex absolute value: $|A+iB| = (A^2+B^2)^{\frac{1}{2}}$

Complex square: $(A+iB)^2 = (A^2-B^2)+i(2AB)$

Complex square root:

$$(A+iB)^{\frac{1}{2}} = \sqrt{\frac{A+(A^2+B^2)^{\frac{1}{2}}}{2}} + \,_2\sqrt{\frac{i\quad B}{\frac{A+(A^2+B^2)^{\frac{1}{2}}}{2}}}$$

Complex natural log: $Ln(A+iB) = Ln((A^2+B^2)^{\frac{1}{2}})+ i$ (ARCTAN B/A)

Complex exponent: $e^{(A+iB)}= e^A(COSB+iSINB)$

Note: all trig functions are assumed to be in the radian mode.

Complex Add:

```
5 REM COMPLEX ADD
10 LET A=A1+A2
20 LET B=B1+B2
30 RETURN
```

Complex Subtraction:

```
5 REM COMPLEX SUBTRACTION
10 LET A=A1-A2
20 LET B=B1-B2
30 RETURN
```

Complex Multiplication:

```
5 REM COMPLEX MULTIPLICATION
10 LET A=(A1*A2)-(B1*B2)
20 LET B=(A1*B2)+(A2*B1)
30 RETURN
```

Complex Division:

```
 5 REM COMPLEX DIVISION
10 LET A=((A1*A2)+(B1*B2))/(A2*A2+B2*B2)
20 LET B=((A2*B1)-(A1*B2))/(A2*A2+B2*B2)
30 RETURN
```

Complex Reciprocal:

```
 5 REM COMPLEX RECIPROCAL
10 LET A=A1/(A1*A1+B1*B1)
20 LET B=-B1/(A1*A1+B1*B1)
30 RETURN
```

Complex Absolute:

```
 5 REM COMPLEX ABSOLUTE
10 LET C=SQR(A1*A1+A2*A2)
20 RETURN
```

Complex Square:

```
 5 REM COMPLEX SQUARE
10 A=A1*A1-A2*A2
20 B=2*A1*A2
30 RETURN
```

Complex Square Root:

```
 5 REM COMPLEX SQUARE ROOT
10 LET A=SQR((A1+SQR(A1*A1+A2*A2))/2)
20 LET B=2*SQR((A1+SQR(A1*A1+A2*A2))/2)
30 LET B=A2/B
40 RETURN
```

Complex Natural Log:

```
 5 REM COMPLEX NATURAL LOG
10 LET A=LOG(SQR(A1*A1+A2*A2))
20 LET B=ATN(A2/A1)
30 RETURN
```

Complex Exponential:

```
 5 REM COMPLEX EXPONENTIAL
10 LET A=EXP(A1)*COS(A2)
20 LET B=EXP(A1)*SIN(A2)
30 RETURN
```

Test Run For Complex Add

```
RUN
INPUT VARIABLES:
```

```
1,0,2,0,
1,1,2,1
1,2,3,4
5,6,7,8
9,10,11,12
13,14,15,16
RESULTS OF SUBROUTINE:
OUTPUT
3,0
3,2
4,6
12,14
20,22
28,30
RUN TERMINATED
END*
```

Test Run For Complex Subtract

```
RUN
INPUT VARIABLES:
1,0,2,0
1,1,2,1
1,2,3,4
11,7,3,5
15,19,31,6
73,10,42,25
RESULTS OF SUBROUTINE:
OUTPUT
−1,0
−1,0
−2,−2
8,2
−16,13
31,−15
RUN TERMINATED
END*
```

Test Run For Complex Multiply

```
RUN
INPUT VARIABLES:
1,0,2,0
1,1,2,1
1,1,4,7
12,15,27,32
2,9,1,7
RESULTS OF SUBROUTINE:
OUTPUT
2,0
1,3
−3,11
−156,789
−61,23
RUN TERMINATED
END*
```

Test Run For Complex Divide

RUN
INPUT VARIABLES:
2,0,1,0
1,1,2,1
4,7,1,1
12,15,27,32
1,1,1,1
RESULTS OF SUBROUTINE:
OUTPUT
2,0
0.6,0.2
5.5,1.5
0.46,0.11
1,0
RUN TERMINATED
END*

Test Run For Complex Reciprocal

RUN
INPUT VARIABLES:
1,0
1,1
2,3
4,5
6,7
RESULTS OF SUBROUTINE:
OUTPUT
1,0
0.5,−0.5
0.15,−0.23
−0.01,−0.04
−0.004,−0.001
RUN TERMINATED
END*

Test Run For Complex Absolute

RUN
INPUT VARIABLES:
1,0
1,1
2,3
4,5
6,7
8,9
RESULTS OF SUBROUTINE:
OUTPUT
1
1.414
3.605
6.403
9.219
12.04
RUN TERMINATED
END*

114

Test Run For Complex Square

```
RUN
INPUT VARIABLES:
1,0
1,1
1,2
3,4
4,5
6,7
8,9
RESULTS OF SUBROUTINE:
OUTPUT
1,0
0,2
−3,4
−7,24
−9,40
−13,84
−17,144
RUN TERMINATED
END*
```

Test Run For Complex Square Root

```
RUN
INPUT VARIABLES:
1,0
1,1
1,2
3,4
5,6
7,8
RESULTS OF SUBROUTINE:
OUTPUT
1,0
1.09,0.45
1.27,0.78
2,1
2.53,1.18
2.97,1.35
RUN TERMINATED
END*
```

Test Run For Complex Log

```
RUN
INPUT VARIABLES:
1,0
1,1
1,2
3,4
5,6
RESULTS OF SUBROUTINE:
OUTPUT
0,0
0.34,0.79
0.80,1.10
```

1.60,0.93
2.05,0.88
RUN TERMINATED
END*

Test Run For Complex Exponential

RUN
INPUT VARIABLES:
1,0
1,1
1,2
3,4
5,6
RESULTS OF SUBROUTINE:
OUTPUT
2.72,0
1.47,2.29
−1.13,2.47
−13.13,−15.20
142.50,−41.47
RUN TERMINATED
END*

DERIVATIVES

The derivative of a function is the limit, if it exists independently of the path by which X approaches X_0 of the difference quotient. Therefore:

$$f'(X) = \lim_{X \to X_0} \frac{f(X) - f(X_0)}{X - X_0}$$

Another, simpler to understand format is: Given a curve $f(X)$ the derivative $f'(X)$ describes the slope of $f(X)$ at X.

The derivatives in this book are the most commonly used or needed in physics, electronics and mathematics.

Purpose: To compute the derivatives of the following functions:

ln X	$\sec^{-1}X$
sin X	$\csc^{-1}X$
tan X	$\sinh^{-1}X$
cot X	$\cosh^{-1}X$
$\sin^{-1}X$	$\tanh^{-1}X$
$\cos^{-1}X$	$\coth^{-1}X$
$\tan^{-1}X$	$\text{sech}^{-1}X$
cot X	$\text{cosech}^{-1}X$

Variables needed: X (the independent variable of the function being differentiated).

116

Variables altered: None.
Variables returned: D (the resultant derivative).
Sources:

```
10 REM DERIVATIVE OF LN(X)
20 LET D=1/X
30 RETURN
```

```
10 REM DERIVATIVE OF SIN(X)
20 LET D=COS(X)
30 RETURN
```

```
10 REM DERIVATIVE OF TAN(X)
20 LET D=1+TAN(X)↑2
30 RETURN
```

```
10 REM DERIVATIVE OF COT(X)
20 LET D=-(1+(1/TAN(X)↑2)))
30 RETURN
```

```
10 REM DERIVATIVE OF ASIN(X)
20 LET D=SQR(1-X*X)
30 RETURN
```

```
10 REM DERIVATIVE OF ACOS(X)
20 LET D=-SQR(1-X*X)
30 RETURN
```

```
10 REM DERIVATIVE OF ATAN(X)
20 LET D=1/(1+X*X)
30 RETURN
```

```
10 REM DERIVATIVE OF ACOT (X)
20 LET D=-1/(X*X+1)
30 RETURN
```

```
10 REM DERIVATIVE OF ASEC(X)
20 LET D=1/(X*SQR(X*X-1))
30 RETURN
```

```
10 REM DERIVATIVE OF ACSC(X)
20 LET D=-1/(X*SQR(X*X-1))
30 RETURN
```

```
10 REM DERIVATIVE OF ASINH(X)
20 LET D=1/SQR(1+X*X)
30 RETURN
```

```
10 REM DERIVATIVE OF ACOSH(X)
20 LET D=1/SQR(X*X-1)
30 RETURN
```

```
10 REM DERIVATIVE OF ATANH(X)
20 LET D=1/(1-X*X)
30 RETURN
```

```
10 REM DERIVATIVE OF ACOTH(X)
20 LET D=-1/(X*X-1)
30 RETURN

10 REM DERIVATIVE OF ASECH(X)
20 LET D=-1/(X*SQR(1-X*X))
30 RETURN

10 REM DERIVATIVE OF ACOSECH(X)
20 LET D=-1/(X*SQR(1+X*X))
30 RETURN
```

Test Run For LN(X) Derivative

```
RUN
INPUT VARIABLES:
?1
?2
?3
?4
?1000
?25
?1.7
?.2
?.1
?107
RESULTS:
OUTPUT
INPUT    OUTPUT
1        1.0000000
2        0.5000000
3        0.3333333
4        0.2500000
1000     1.0E-03
25       4.0E-02
1.7      0.5882353
.2       5.0000000
.1       10.000000
107      9.345E-03
RUN COMPLETE
END*
```

Test Run For SIN(X) Derivative

```
RUN
INPUT VARIABLES:
?1
?3
?5
?7
?9
?11
?13
?15
?17
?.1
RESULTS:
```

```
OUTPUT
INPUT    OUTPUT
1        0.5403023
3        -0.9899925
5        0.2836622
7        0.7539023
9        -0.9111302
11       4.425E-03
13       0.9074468
15       -0.7596879
17       -0.2751633
.1       0.9950042
RUN COMPLETE
END*
```

Test Run For TAN(X) Derivative

```
RUN
INPUT VARIABLES:
?.1
?.2
?.3
?.4
?.5
?1
?2
?3
?4
RESULTS:
OUTPUT
INPUT    OUTPUT
.1       1.0100670
.2       1.0410914
.3       1.0956889
.4       1.1787541
.5       1.2984464
1        3.4255188
2        5.7743992
3        1.0203195
4        2.3405501
RUN COMPLETE
END*
```

Test Run For COT(X) Derivative

```
RUN
INPUT VARIABLES:
?.1
?.2
?.3
?.4
?.5
?1
?2
?3
?4
RESULTS:
OUTPUT
```

INPUT	OUTPUT
.1	100.33400
.2	25.336017
.3	11.450531
.4	6.5942771
.5	4.3506853
1	1.4122829
2	1.2094504
3	50.213768
4	1.7459624

```
RUN COMPLETE
END*
```

Test Run For ACOS(X) Derivative

```
RUN
INPUT VARIABLES:
?.6
?.7
?.8
?.9
?.95
?1
?.15
RESULTS:
OUTPUT
```

INPUT	OUTPUT
.6	−0.8000000
.7	−0.7141428
.8	−0.6000000
.9	−0.4358899
.95	−0.3122499
1	0.0000000
.15	−0.9886860

```
RUN COMPLETE
END*
```

Test Run For ASIN(X) Derivative

```
RUN
INPUT VARIABLES:
?.1
?.2
?.3
?.4
?.5
?.6
?.7
?1
?.8
RESULTS:
OUTPUT
```

INPUT	OUTPUT
.1	0.9949874
.2	0.9797959
.3	0.9539392
.4	0.9165151
.5	0.8660254
.6	0.8000000
.7	0.7141428
1	0.0000000
.8	0.6000000

```
RUN COMPLETE
END*
```

Test Run For ATAN(X) Derivative

```
RUN
INPUT VARIABLES:
?0
?.1
?.2
?.3
?.4
?.5
?.6
?.7
?.8
?.9
RESULTS:
OUTPUT
```

INPUT	OUTPUT
0	1.0000000
.1	0.9900990
.2	0.9615385
.3	0.9174311
.4	0.8620600
.5	0.8000000
.6	0.7352941
.7	0.6711409
.8	0.6097561
.9	0.5524862

```
RUN COMPLETE
END*
```

Test Run For ACOT(X) Derivative

```
RUN
INPUT VARIABLES:
?.9
?.8
?.7
?.6
?.5
?.4
?.3
?.2
?.1
?0
RESULTS:
OUTPUT
```

INPUT	OUTPUT
.9	−0.5524862
.8	−0.6097561
.7	−0.6711409
.6	−0.7352941
.5	−0.8000000
.4	−0.8620690
.3	−0.9174311
.2	−0.9615385
.1	−0.9900990
0	−1.0000000

```
RUN COMPLETE
END*
```

Test Run For ASEC(X) Derivative

```
RUN
INPUT VARIABLES:
?2
?3
?4
?5
?6
?7
RESULTS:
OUTPUT
```

INPUT	OUTPUT
2	0.2886751
3	0.1178511
4	6.454E-02
5	4.082E-02
6	2.817E-02
7	2.061E-02

```
RUN COMPLETE
END*
```

Test Run For ACS(X) Derivative

```
RUN
INPUT VARIABLES:
?3
?4
```

```
?5
?6
?7
?8
RESULTS:
OUTPUT
```

INPUT	OUTPUT
3	−0.1178511
4	−6.454E-02
5	−4.082E-02
6	−2.817E-02
7	−2.061E-02
8	−1.574E-02

```
RUN COMPLETE
END*
```

Test Run For ASINH(X) Derivative

```
RUN
INPUT VARIABLES:
?1
?2
?3
?4
?5
?6
?7
?8
RESULTS:
OUTPUT
```

INPUT	OUTPUT
1	0.7071068
2	0.4472136
3	0.3162278
4	0.2425356
5	0.1961161
6	0.1643990
7	0.1414214
8	0.1240347

```
RUN COMPLETE
END*
```

Test Run For ACOSH(X) Derivative

```
RUN
INPUT VARIABLES:
?2
?3
?4
?5
?6
?7
RESULTS:
OUTPUT
```

INPUT	OUTPUT
2	0.5773502
3	0.3535534
4	0.2581890

5	0.2041241
6	0.6190309
7	0.1443376

RUN COMPLETE
END*

Test Run For ATANH(X) Derivative

RUN
INPUT VARIABLES:
?.9
?.8
?.7
?.6
?.5
?.4
?.3
?.2
?.1
RESULTS:
OUTPUT

INPUT	OUTPUT
.9	5.2631579
.8	2.7777778
.7	1.9607843
.6	1.5625000
.5	1.3333333
.4	1.1904761
.3	1.0989011
.2	1.0416667
.1	1.0101010

RUN COMPLETE
END*

Test Run For ACOTH(X) Derivative

RUN
INPUT VARIABLES:
?.1
?.2
?.3
?.4
?.5
?.6
?.7
?.8
?.9
RESULTS:
OUTPUT

INPUT	OUTPUT
.1	1.0101010
.2	1.4166667
.3	1.0989011
.4	1.1904761
.5	1.3333333
.6	1.5625000
.7	1.9607843
.8	2.7777778
.9	5.2631579

RUN COMPLETE

END*

Test Run For ASECH(X) Derivative

RUN
INPUT VARIABLES:
?.1
?.2
?.3
?.4
?.5
?.6
?.8
?.9
?.7
?2.0
RESULTS:
OUTPUT

INPUT	OUTPUT
.1	10.050378
.2	5.1031036
.3	3.4942828
.4	2.7277236
.5	2.3094011
.6	2.0833333
.8	2.0833333
.9	2.5490637
.7	2.0004000
2.0	0.7071068

RUN COMPLETE
END*

Test Run For ACOSECH(X) Derivative

RUN
INPUT VARIABLES:
?.1
?.2
?.3
?.4
?.5
?.6
?.7
?.8
RESULTS:
OUTPUT

INPUT	OUTPUT
.1	9.9503719
.2	4.8076923
.3	3.1927543
.4	2.1551724
.5	1.2254902
.6	1.1703313
.7	0.7621951
.8	0.8258824

RUN COMPLETE
END*

EXPONENTS

When using logarithms (see logarithms) you will sometimes need to find the log of a given number, using one base, in another base or to convert exponents. Example:

$$2^{50}=10^X$$

Using the exponent conversion, you can deduce that X is 15.05149978. In other words:

$$2^{63}=10^{18.965}$$

A 64-bit number has one bit for the sign and 63 bits for the number. Therefore, the maximum magnitude is 2^{63} or 63 binary digits. How many digits is that in decimal? Answer: 19 digits.

Purpose: To convert exponents or to solve for an unknown exponent in the following formula $a^x = b^c$, where a,b,c are known.

Variables needed: A (first base). B (exponent of first base). C (second base).

Variables altered: None.

Variables returned: D (exponent of second base).

Equations:

$$d= \frac{bLoga}{Logc} \quad \text{where } a^b=c^d$$

Source:
```
 5 REM EXPONENTS
10 LET D=(B*LOG(A))/LOG(C)
20 RETURN
```

TEST RUN FOR EXPONENTS

```
RUN
INPUT VARIABLES:
?2,3,10
?10,3,2
?2,4,10
?10,4,2
?2,5,10
?10,5,2
?2,6,10
?10,6,2
?2,7,10
?10,7,2
RESULTS:
OUTPUT
```

INPUT	OUTPUT
2 3 10	0.9031000
10 3 2	9.9658000

```
 2 4 10    1.2041000
10 4  2   13.287700
 2 5 10    1.5051000
10 5  2   16.609600
 2 6 10    1.8062000
10 6  2   19.931600
 2 7 10    2.1072000
10 7  2   23.253500
RUN COMPLETE
END*
```

FACTORIALS

If n is a positive integer (a whole number greater than zero) factorial n is the product $1 \cdot 2 \cdot 3 \ldots \ldots n$. This number is written as n!

Factorials are often used in statistics. Some of these uses are:

—Permutations (written P_n^m) are the number of arrangements possible to m objects when selected n at a time. This can be calculated as: $m!/((m-n)!)$

—Combinations (written C_n^m) are the number of arrangements possible, if the actual sequence is ignored, to m objects selected n at a time. This can be calculated as: $m!/(n!((m-n)!))$.

EXAMPLES OF FACTORIALS

```
1!=1
2!=2
3!=6
4!=24
5!=120
6!=720
7!=5040
8!=40320
9!=362880
10!=3628800
11!=39916800
12!=479001600
13!=6227020800
```

Purpose: Find the factorial of a number.
Variables needed: X (the number to find the factorial of).
Variables altered: I.
Variables returned: Z(X!).
Source:

```
 5 REM FACTORIAL
10 LET Z=1
20 FOR I=1 TO X
30 LET Z=Z*I
40 NEXT I
50 RETURN
```

Test Run For Factorials

RUN
INPUT VARIABLES:

```
?0
?2
?4
?6
?8
?10
?12
?14
RESULTS:
OUTPUT
INPUT    OUTPUT
0        1.0000000
2        2.0000000
4        24.000000
6        720.00000
8        40320.000
10       3628800.0
12       4.790016E08
14       8.717829E10
RUN COMPLETE
END*
```

LOGARITHMS

Any positive number (A) can be expressed as one number (any positive number greater than one) raised to the power of another number (positive, zero or negative):

$$A=B^C$$

This function can be reversed (the inverse of an exponent-type function is called a logarithm) and shown as:

$$\log^B A=C$$

where C is the logarithm of A to base B.

BASIC has a function called **LOG** which gives the log of a number to the base e (2.71828 . . .). This is called the *natural* or *naperian* logarithm of a number.

LOGS ANY BASE

Purpose: To calculate the log of any number of any base.
Variables needed: X (the base desired). Z (the argument of the log function).
Variables altered: None.
Variables returned: Y (the value of the log function).
Equations:

$$\log_x{}^Z = \frac{\log^Z}{\log^X}$$

Source:
```
 5 REM LOG ANY BASE
10 LET Y=LOG(Z)/LOG(X)
20 RETURN
```

124

Test Run For Logs Any Base

```
RUN
INPUT VARIABLES:
2,1
2,2
2,3
2,4
2,5
2,6
10,1
10,2
10,3
12,4
15,7
RESULTS OF SUBROUTINE:
OUTPUT
0.0000000
1.0000000
1.5849625
2.0000000
2.3219281
2,5849625
0.0000000
0.3010300
0.4771213
0.5578859
0.7185650
RUN TERMINATED
END*
```

PERCENTAGE CHANGE FROM Y TO X

Purpose: To find the percentage change from a variable going from y-value to an x-value.

Variables needed: X (x-value). Y (y-value).

Variables altered: None.

Variable returned: C(% change).

Equations: $\dfrac{(X-Y)100}{Y} = \%$ change

Source:
```
 5 REM % CHANGE
10 LET C=((X-)*100)/Y
20 RETURN
```

Test Run For Percentage Change

```
RUN
INPUT VARIABLES:
1,1
2,1
```

3,1
4,1
5,2
6,2
7,2
8,3
9,3
10,3
11,3
RESULTS OF SUBROUTINE:
OUTPUT
 0.0000000
 100.00000
 200.00000
 300.00000
 150.00000
 200.00000
 250.00000
 166.66667
 200.00000
 233.33333
 266.66667
RUN TERMINATED
END*

Chapter 10
Physics

The programs in this chapter concern motion and matter.

ALTITUDE IN FEET

Purpose: To find the altitude in feet when you know the barometric pressure in inches of mercury (standard measure).
Variables needed: P (barometric pressure).
Variables altered: None.
Variables returned: A (altitude).
Equations: $A = \dfrac{25000 \text{Ln} 30}{P}$

Source:

```
 5 REM ALTITUDE IN FEET
 6 REM ACCURACY DECREASES AFTER 60,000 FEET
10 LET A/25000*LOG (30/P)
20 RETURN
```

Test Run For Altitude In Feet

```
RUN
INPUT VARIABLES:
?30
?10
?15
?29.5
?21.52
RESULTS:
INPUT      OUTPUT
30         0.0000000
10         27465.307
15         17328.680
29.5       420.17796
21.52      8305.3662
RUN COMPLETE
END*
```

127

ANGULAR VELOCITY

Purpose: To compute the angular velocity when the frequency is known.

Variables needed: F (Frequency in hertz).

Variables altered: None.

Variables returned: W (angular velocity).

Equations: $W = 2\pi f$

Source:
```
 5 REM ANGULAR VELOCITY
10 LET W=6.28319*F
20 RETURN
```

Test Run For Angular Velocity

```
RUN.
INPUT VARIABLES:
?2.5
?5
?10
?20
?40
RESULTS:
```

INPUT	OUTPUT
2.5	15.707975
5	31.415950
10	62.831900
20	125.66380
40	251.32760

```
RUN COMPLETE
END*
```

Distance

Purpose: To compute the distance a body will travel.

Variables needed: V (initial velocity). T (travel time). A (acceleration rate).

Variables altered: None.

Variables returned: D (distance travelled).

Equations: $D/VT + \frac{1}{2}AT^2$

Source:
```
 5 REM DISTANCE
10 LET D = (V*T)+((A*T*T)/2)
20 RETURN
```

Test Run For Distance

```
RUN
INPUT VARIABLES:
?1,1,1
?1,2,2
?1,3,3
?1,4,4
```

```
?1,5,5
?2,1,1
?2,2,2
?2,3,3
RESULTS:
OUTPUT
INPUT   OUTPUT
1 1 1   1.5000000
1 2 2   6.0000000
1 3 3    16.500000
1 4 4   36.000000
1 5 5   67.500000
2 1 1   2.5000000
2 2 2   8.0000000
2 3 3   19.500000
RUN COMPLETE
END*
```

Falling Object In Feet

Purpose: To find the time required for an object to fall X number of feet.

Variables needed: D (height in feet).

Variables altered: None.

Variables returned: T (time in seconds to fall).

Equation: $t = (2d/32.174\,\text{fts}^{-2})^{1/2}$ Air friction is not taken into account.

Source:

```
5 REM ALTITUDE IN FEET TIME TO FALL
10 LET T = SQR(2*D/32.174)
20 RETURN
```

Test Run For Falling Object In Feet

```
RUN
INPUT VARIABLES:
?1
?4
?9
?16
?25
?36
?49
RESULTS:
OUTPUT
INPUT   OUTPUT
1       0.2493230
4       0.4976461
9       0.7479692
16      0.9972923
25      1.2466154
36      1.4959384
49      1.7452615
RUN COMPLETE
END*
```

FALLING OBJECT IN METERS

Purpose: To find the time required for an object to fall X number of meters.

Variables needed: D (height in meters).

Variables altered: None.

Variables returned: T (time in seconds to fall).

Equation: $t = (2d/9.8 \text{ ms}^{-2})^{\frac{1}{2}}$

Air friction is not taken into account.

Source:

```
5 REM ALTITUDE IN METERS TIME TO FALL
10 LET T = SQR(2*D/9.8)
20 RETURN
```

Test Run For Falling Object In Meters

```
RUN
INPUT VARIABLES:
?1
?4
?9
?16
?25
?36
?49
?64
?81
RESULTS:
OUTPUT
1      0.4517500
4      0.9035079
9      1.3552619
16     1.8070158
25     2.2587698
36     2.7105237
49     3.1622777
64     3.6140316
81     4.0657856

RUN COMPLETE
END*
```

Chapter 11
Random Numbers

When random numbers are scanned they show no discernible pattern in their sequence. Random numbers are often used in programs that involve sampling data (Monte Carlo Method), simulating events and playing games.

RANDOM NUMBER GENERATOR—UNIFORM DISTRIBUTION

Purpose: To generate random numbers under programmer control (RND statement does not always give adequate control). This routine generates approximately 100,000 random numbers in the range 0 to 1 with a uniform distribution. A sequence of numbers can be repeated by saving and restoring X.

Variables Needed: X (controls random sequence).

Variables Altered: X1 (a work variables).

Variables Returned: X (new value, re-enter for next number).

Source:

```
 5 REM UNIFORM RANDOM NUMBERS
10 X1= (24298*X+99991) /199017
20 X = X1-INT (X1)
30 RETURN
```

Test Run For Random Number (Uniform)

```
RUN
INPUT VARIABLES
12345 'seed
```

RESULTS OF SUBROUTINE:
OUTPUT
0.7043701
0.8636859
0.7635244
0.3187395
0.7456843
0.9876821
0.8453889
0.1819763
0.3876525
0.2876493
RUN TERMINATED
END*

RANDOM NUMBER GENERATOR—NORMALIZED DISTRIBUTION

Purpose: To generate a series of random numbers in the range of 0 to 1 with a "normal" distribution, given a previous value (or seed) and the standard deviation.

Two routines are shown (the mean is always ½ or 0.5):

—Using the standard RND function—(which should produce a number between 0 to 1 with a uniform distribution.

—Using the controlled generator—in cases where the generated number of RND is not desirable because it is uncontrollable.

Variables Needed: Routine A: S (standard deviation). Routine B: S (standard deviation). X (previous value or if it is the first time a seed or starting value)

Variables Altered: X1 (work variable). X2 (work variable). X3 (unadjusted random number).

Variables Returned: X (the normally-distributed random value).

Source:

Routine A

```
 5 REM UNCONTROLLED NORMAL RANDOM
10 ×1 = RND
20 ×2 = RND
30 ×3 = 2* LOG (X1)
40 ×3 = SQR (ABS(X3))
50 X3 = X3*COS (X2* 6.2831853)
60 X  = X3*S + 0.5
70 RETURN
```

Test Run For Random Number-Normal (A)

RUN
INPUT VARIABLES:
0.1 'sigma
RESULTS OF SUBROUTINE:
OUTPUT
0.4439
0.5676

0.6247
0.4309
0.5097
0.4766
0.4343
0.4813
0.4567
0.6290
RUN TERMINATED
END*

Routine B

```
 5 REM CONTROLLED NORMAL RANDOM
10 X1 = (24298* X + 99991)/199017
20 X1 = X1 − 1NT (X1)
30 X2=(24298*X+99991)/99017
40 X2 = X2 INT (X2)
50 X3 = 2*LOG(X1)
60 X3 = SQR (ABS (X))
70 X3 = X3* COS(X2*6.2831853)
80 X  = X3*S + 0.5
90 RETURN
```

Test Run For Random Number-Normal (B)

RUN
INPUT VARIABLES:
12345 'seed
0.1 'sigma
RESULTS OF SUBROUTINE:
OUTPUT
0.4583
0.4474
0.4883
0.3625
0.4950
0.5016
0.4592
0.4683
0.6819
0.3792
0.3892
RUN TERMINATED
END

Chapter 12
Sequencing Routine

Purpose: It is sometimes necessary to place a table of values into sequence for later use. This routine does so by "tricking" the lower values upwards (sometimes known as bubble sorting). This technique, while considered inefficient, is the simplest and most foolproof of the internal sorts. Unless extreme speed or repetitive sorting is a problem, you will find this routine more than adequate.

Variables Needed: T (the table to be sequenced). N (the size of the table).

Variables Altered: U (upper end—or low value—locator). H (temporary storage). B (lower end—or high value—locator). L (temporary storage).

Variables Returned: T (the sequenced table).

Source:

```
 1 REM THIS ROUTINE SEQUENCES A TABLE T
 2 REM OF LENGTH N INTO ASCENDING
 3 REM SEQUENCE
10 FOR U = 1 TO N-1
20 LET L = U + 1
30 FOR B = N TO 1 step -1
40 IF T(B) > T(U) THEN 80
50 LET H = T(U)
60 LET T (U) = T(B)
70 LET T (B) = H
80 NEXT B
90 NEXT U
100 RETURN
```

Test Run For Sequencing Routine

```
RUN
INPUT VARIABLES:
7 'count
6
7
5
4
1
3
2
RESULTS OF SUBROUTINE:
OUTPUT
1
2
3
4
5
6
7
RUN TERMINATED
END
```

SEQUENTIAL SEARCH

Purpose: This routine searches a table for a given value. The table can be in any order. It returns the location of the found value in the table or zero if it is not found. The average search time is proportional to $N/2$ and the maximum to N. For short tables this method of searching is preferred. For unsequenced tables this method is necessary.

Variables Needed: X (value to find). T (table to search). N (size of table).

Variables Altered: I (loop counter)

Variables Returned: L (location of value)

Source:

```
 1 REM THIS ROUTINE SEARCHES A TABLE
 2 REM OF VALUES AND RETURNS THE
 3 REM LOCATION OF A MATCHING VALUE
 4 REM OR ZERO IF NOT FOUND IN THE TABLE
 5 REM SEARCH IS SEQUENTIAL AND DOES
 6 REM NOT REQUIRE A SEQUENTIAL TABLE
10 LET L = 0
20 FOR 1 = 1 TO N
30 IF X <> T(1) THEN 60
40 LET L = I
50 GOTO 70
60 NEXT 1
70 RETURN
```

Test Run For Sequential Search

```
RUN
INPUT VARIABLES:
9 'size
3
2
4
7
9
11
15
17
12
2 'search for
4
15
RESULTS OF SUBROUTINE :
OUTPUT
2
3
7
RUN TERMINATED
END*
```

Chapter 13
Trajectories

When you write programs for model rockets, bullets fired from a gun, cars leaving a ramp, baseballs or a stream of water from a hose it is sometimes necessary to find the altitude and range (distance travelled by the object).

The height (or altitude) the object can reach and the distance it can travel can be calculated as follows:

Altitude: where A is the height or altitude reached. V is the speed of the object (velocity). θ is the angle, relative to the ground at which the object leaves. g is the acceleration due to gravity. See Fig. 13-1.

$$A = \frac{V^2 \sin\theta}{2g}$$

Range: where R is the range.

$$R = \frac{V^2 \sin^2}{g}$$

Time of Flight: Where T is the time in seconds.

$$T = \frac{2V}{g}(\sin\theta)^{1/2}$$

CENTIMETERS PER SECOND (cm/s)

Purpose: To calculate how far an object will travel in centimeters, given the speed (or velocity) in centimeters per second and the time in the air.

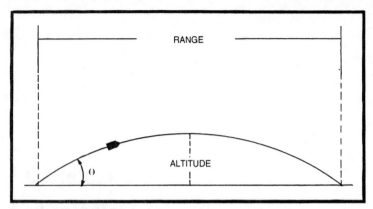

Fig. 13-1. Determining the altitude and range of an object.

Variables needed: T (angle in degrees) V (speed or velocity in centimeters per second).

Variables altered: None.

Variables returned: R (range in centimeters). A (altitude in centimeters). S (time of flight in seconds).

Note: To obtain the range in kilometers or the altitude in kilometers, divide altitude or range by 100,000 (one hundred thousand).

Source:

Range

```
 5 REM CENTIMETERS PER SECOND—RANGE
10 LET R = SIN (T* 3.49E—02)* V*V*1.0194E-03
20 RETURN
```

Altitude

```
 5 REM CENTIMETERS PER SECOND—ALTITUDE
10 LET A= SIN(T*1.745E-02)*V*V*5.097E-04
20 RETURN
```

Time

```
 5 REM TIME OF FLIGHT FOR CM/SEC
10 LET S = SQR(SIN(T*1.745E-02))*V*2.039E-03
20 RETURN
```

Test Run For Trajectories (CMSRange)

```
RUN
INPUT VARIABLES:
5,100
10,100
15,100
30,100
```

45,100
75,100
RESULTS OF SUBROUTINE :
OUTPUT
1.7691445
3.4845547
5.0941283
8.8237922
10.190000
5.0993578
RUN TERMINATED
END*

Test Run For Trajectories (CMS-Altitude)

RUN
INPUT VARIABLES:
5,100
10,100
15,100
30,100
45,100
75,100
RESULTS OF SUBROUTINE:
OUTPUT
0.4441492
0.8849195
1.3189575
2.5480640
3.6035892
4.9229980
RUN TERMINATED
END*

Test Run For Trajectories (CMS-Time)

RUN
INPUT VARIABLES:
5,100
10,100
15,100
30,100
45,100
75,100
RESULTS OF SUBROUTINE:
OUTPUT
0.0601900
0.0849595
0.1037231
0.1441667
0.1714461
0.2003894
RUN TERMINATED
END*

FEET PER SECOND

Purpose: To compute a projectile's motion given the speed in feet per second and the angle in degree, including the time in the air.

139

Variables needed: T (angle of take off in degrees). V (speed or velocity in feet per second).

Variables altered: None.

Variables returned: R (range in feet). A (maximum altitude in feet). S (time in the air in seconds).

Source:

Range

```
 5 REM FEET PER SECOND—RANGE
10 LET R = SIN (T* 3.49E-02) *V*V*3.0864E-02
20 RETURN
```

Altitude

```
 5 REM FEET PER SECOND—ALTITUDE
10 LET A = SIN(T* 1.745E-02)
20 RETURN
```

Time

```
 5 REM FEET PER SECOND—TIME
10 LET S = SQR(SIN(T *1.745E-02))*V*6.173E-02
20 RETURN
```

Test Run For Trajectories Feet— Range

```
RUN
INPUT VARIABLES:
5,100
10,100
15,100
30,100
45,100
75,100
RESULTS OF SUBROUTINE:
OUTPUT
53.584766
105.54200
154.29360
267.25959
308.63999
154.45199
RUN TERMINATED
END*
```

Test Run For Trajectories Feet-Altitude

```
RUN
INPUT VARIABLES:
5,100
10,100
15,100
30,100
45,100
75,100
RESULTS OF SUBROUTINE:
```

```
OUTPUT
13.447343
26.792383
39.933593
77.146799
109.10455
149.05181
RUN TERMINATED
END*
```

Test Run For Trajectories Feet-Time

```
RUN
INPUT VARIABLES:
5,100
10,100
15,100
30,100
45,100
75,100
RESULTS OF SUBROUTINE:
OUTPUT
1.8222309
2.5721177
3.1401787
4.3645967
5.1904690
6.0667178
RUN TERMINATED
END*
```

KILOMETERS PER HOUR (km/hr)

Purpose: To compute the projectile motion in kilometers, given the speed in kilometers per hour and the angle in degrees and the time in the air.

Variables Needed: T (angle in degrees). V (speed in kilometers per hour).

Variables Altered: None.

Variables Returned: R (range in kilometers). A(altitude in kilometers). S (time of flight in seconds).

Source:

Range

```
5 REM RANGE IN KILOMETERS FROM KM/HR
10 LET R = SIN(T* 3.49E-02) *V*V*7.866E-06
20 RETURN
```

Altitude

```
5 REM ALTITUDE FROM KM/HR IN KILOMETERS
10 LET A = SIN (T*1.745E-02) *V*V*3.933E-06
20 RETURN
```

Time

```
 5 REM TIME IN SECONDS FROM KM/HR
10 LET S = SQR(SIN(T*1.745E-02))*V*5.663E-02
20 RETURN
```

Test Run For Trajectories (KM—Range)

```
RUN
INPUT VARIABLES:
5,100
10,100
15,100
30,100
45,100
75,100
RESULTS OF SUBROUTINE:
OUTPUT
0.0136566
0.0268984
0.0393233
0.0681138
0.0786600
0.0393636
RUN TERMINATED
END*
```

Test Run For Trajectories (KM-Altitude)

```
RUN
INPUT VARIABLES:
5,100
10,100
15,100
30,100
45,100
75,100
RESULTS OF SUBROUTINE:
OUTPUT
0.0034272
0.0068283
0.0101775
0.0196616
0.0278064
0.0379873
RUN TERMINATED
END*
```

Test Run For Trajectories KM-Time

```
RUN
INPUT VARIABLES:
5,100
10,100
15,100
30,100
```

45,100
75,100
RESULTS OF SUBROUTINE:
OUTPUT
1.6716821
2.3596149
2.8807439
4.0040031
4.7616436
5.5654986
RUN TERMINATED
END*

MILES PER HOUR (MPH)

Purpose: To compute the projectile's travel, in miles, given the speed in miles per hour, the angle in degrees and the time of flight.

Variables needed: T (angle in degrees). V (speed in miles per hour).

Variables altered: None.

Variables returned: R (range in miles). A (altitude in miles). S (time of flight in seconds).

Source:

Range

```
5 REM RANGE IN MILES FROM MPH
10 LET R = SIN(T*3.49E-02)*V*V*1.2574E-05
20 RETURN
```

Altitude

```
5 REM ALTITUDE IN MILES FROM MPH
10 LET A = SIN(T*1.745E-02)*V*V*6.287E-06
20 RETURN
```

Time

```
5 REM TIME OF FLIGHT FOR MPH
10 LET S = SQR(SIN(T*1.745E-02))*V*9.053E-02
20 RETURN
```

Test Run For Trajectories (MPH-Range)

RUN
INPUT VARIABLES:
5,100
10,100

143

15,100
30,100
45,100
75,100
RESULTS OF SUBROUTINE:
OUTPUT
0.0218304
0.0429978
0.0628592
0.1088816
0.1257400
0.0629238
RUN TERMINATED
END*

Test Run For Trajectories (MPH-Altitude)

RUN
INPUT VARIABLES:
5,100
10,100
15,100
30,100
45,100
75,100
RESULTS OF SUBROUTINE:
OUTPUT
0.0054785
0.0109152
0.0162690
0.314296
0.0444492
0.0607237
RUN TERMINATED
END*

Test Run For Trajectories (MPH—TIME)

RUN
INPUT VARIABLES:
5,100
10,100
15,100
30,100
45,100
75,100
RESULTS OF SUBROUTINE:
OUTPUT
2.6723889
3.7721338
4.6052224
6.4008901
7.6120712
8.8971320
RUN TERMINATED
END*

Chapter 14
Unique Value Generator

Purpose: To generate N number of unique (different) numbers.

Variables needed: V (dimensioned variable before subroutine execution). N (the size of the dimensioned variable V).

Variables altered: I,J (counters used in the FOR-NEXT loops).

Variables returned: V (dimensioned variable of size N).

Source:

```
1 REM GENERATES A TABLE OF UNIQUE (RANDOM) NUMBERS
2 REM THERE ARE NO DUPLICATIONS IN THE LIST
3 REM IDEAL FOR GAME PROGRAMS
4 REM VECTOR V IS DIMENSIONED TO SIZE N BEFORE
5 REM SUBROUTINE EXECUTION
10 FOR I = 1 TO N
15 REM  K STANDS FOR ANY CONSTANT THE USER DESIRES TO USE
16 REM TO ESTABLISH THE RANGE OF THE RANDOM NUMBERS GENER-
   ATED
17 REM THIS PROCEDURE GENERATES RAMDOM NUMBERS RANGING
   FROM
18 REM O TO K (K must be greater than or equal to N)
20 V(I) = 1+INT(K*RND)
30 FOR J = 1 TO I-1
40 IF V(I) = V(J) THEN 20
50 NEXT J
60 NEXT I
70 RETURN
```

Note: In using this subroutine the REMs can be removed. Also, change the line number given in the THEN statement to match the line numbers used in your program.

Test Run For Unique Value Generator

```
RUN
INPUT VARIABLES:
25,100
RESULTS OF SUBROUTINE:
OUTPUT
38
25
73
81
84
24
80
69
40
56
87
2
93
52
28
67
31
49
19
58
92
15
89
62
23
RUN TERMINATED
END*
```

Chapter 15
Values

The programs in the chapter can be used to find or locate maximum or minimum values.

MAXIMUM VALUE FINDER

Purpose: To find and return the largest magnitude value in a table of values. Note: **magnitude** means using unsigned or absolute values so that -77 is "greater" than 27 in terms of magnitude, but lower in terms of value. See histographics as an example of usage.

Variables needed: T (table of values being scanned) N(size of the scanned table).

Variables altered: I (loop control and current-index).

Variables returned: M (maximum magnitude in table).

Source:

```
1 REM FINDS THE LARGEST VALUE
2 REM (ABSOLUTE) IN A TABLE OF
3 REM VALUES
10 LET M = T(1)
20 FOR 1 = 2 TO N
30 IF ABS (T(1)) < M THEN 50
40 LET M = ABS(T(I))
50 NEXT I
60 RETURN
```

Test Run For Maximum Value Finder

```
RUN
INPUT VARIABLES:
10, 1, 2, 3, 7, 5, 6, 12, 15, 22, 2
RESULTS OF SUBROUTINE:
OUTPUT
22
RUN TERMINATED
END*
```

147

MAXIMUM VALUE LOCATOR

Purpose: This routine locates the entry in a table which has the largest magnitude (absolute value).

Variable needed: N (size of table). T (table of DIM(N)).

Variables altered: I (loop counter).

Variables returned: L (location of maximum value).

Source:
```
1 REM FINDS THE LOCATION OF THE
2 REM LARGEST VALUE (ABSOLUTE) IN A
3 REM TABLE OF VALUES. IF MORE THAN
4 REM ONE LOCATION HAS THE MAXIMUM
5 REM VALUE THAN THE LAST IS RETURNED
10 LET L = 1
20 FOR I = 2 TO N
30 IF ABS (T(I)) <ABS(T(I)) THEN 50
40 LET L = 1
50 NEXT 1
60 RETURN
```

Test Run For Maximum Value Locator

```
RUN
INPUT VARIABLES:
10,1,2,3,7,5,6,12, 15,22,2
RESULTS OF SUBROUTINE:
OUTPUT
9
RUN TERMINATED
END*
```

MINIMUM VALUE FINDER

Purpose: To find and return the lowest magnitude value in a table of values. Note that the magnitude is independent of the sign (-98 is "greater" than 40)

Variables needed: T (table to be scanned). N (size of scanned table).

Variables altered: I (scan loop counter).

Variables returned: S (smallest magnitude number found in table).

Source:
```
1 REM FIND THE SMALLEST VALUE
2 REM IN A TABLE OF VALUES
3 REM RESULT IS SMALLEST MAGNITUDE
4 REM OR ABSOLUTE VALUE
10 LET S=T(1)
20 FOR I=2 TO N
30 IF ABS (T(I))>THEN 50
40 LET S=ABS(T(I))
50 NEXT I
60 RETURN
```

Test Run For Minimum Value Finder

```
RUN
INPUT VARIABLES: 15 15,12,11,7,9,3,5,6,22,15,33,10,10,1073.2,99,53

RESULTS OF SUBROUTINE:
OUTPUT
2
RUN TERMINATED
END*
```

MINIMUM VALUE LOCATOR

Purpose: To locate, as an index, the entry in a table which contains the lowest magnitude value. Note: the magnitude depends on the absolute value and that -35 is "greater" than 10 in respect to magnitude.

Variables needed: T (table to be scanned). N (table size or dimension).

Variables altered: I (loop counter used to locate comparison value).

Variables returned: L (location, as an index value, of the smallest value in the table).

Note: If two entries in the table are both the lowest, the location of the first is returned.

Source:
```
 1 REM FINDS THE LOCATION OF THE
 2 REM SMALLEST VALUE IN A TABLE
 3 REM IF TWO VALUES ARE THE SAME
 4 REM THEN THE FIRST IS RETURNED
10 LET L = 1
20 FOR I = 2 TO N
30 IF ABS (T(I))< = ABS(T(L)) THEN 50
40 LET L = I
50 NEXT I
60 RETURN
```

Test Run For Minimum Value Locator

```
RUN
INPUT VARIABLES:
15
15,12,11,7,9,3,5,6,22,15,33,10, 1073, 2, 99
RESULTS OF SUBROUTINE:
OUTPUT
14
RUN TERMINATED
END*
```

Chapter 16
Vectors

A vector is a matrix of n rows and a single column or a single dimensioned variable (or group of variables). In terms of geometry, physics and electronics it can represent directional magnitudes such as forces, velocities, accelerations, displacements and flows.

The two-dimensional vector greatly resembles a complex variable and can be manipulated in a similar fashion, but they are not at all the same.

Adding two vectors together gives a new resultant vector or composite. Subtracting two vectors gives the difference vector. This vector, when added to one of the two original vectors, gives the other vector as the composite vector.

The dot product of two vectors and the cross product are both used extensively in physics.

CROSS PRODUCT OF VECTORS

Purpose: Computes the cross product between two vectors

Variables needed: X1 (x coordinate of 1st vector). X2 (x coordinate of 2nd vector). Y1 (y coordinate of 1st vector). Y2 (y coordinate of 2nd vector). Z1 (z coordinate of 1st vector). Z2 (z coordinate of 2nd vector).

Variables altered: None.

Variables returned: X3 (x coordinate of new vector). Y3 (y coordinate of new vector). Z3 (z coordinate of new vector).

Equations: $\overline{A} \times \overline{B}$ $\quad Y_1 Z_2 - Z_1 Y_2$
$$= Z_1 X_2 - X_1 Z_2.$$
$$X_1 Y_2 - Y_1 X_2.$$

Source:
```
 5 REM COMPUTES CROSS PRODUCT
10 LET X3=(Y1*Z2)-(Z1*Y2)
20 LET Y3=(Z1*X2)-(X1*Z2)
30 LET Z3=(X1*Y2)-(Y1*X2)
40 RETURN
```

Test Run For Vectors Cross-Product

```
RUN
INPUT VARIABLES:
1,2,3,4,5,6
7,8,9,10, 11,12
1,2,3,7,8,9
1,2,3,12,11,10
3,1,2,4,5,6
RESULTS OF SUBROUTINE:
OUTPUT
-3,6,-3
-3,6,-3
-6,12,-6
-13,26,-13
-4,-10,11
RUN TERMINATED
END*
```

DOT PRODUCT OF VECTORS

Purpose: Computes the dot product of two vectors.

Variables needed: X1 (x coordinate 1st vector). Y1 (y coordinate 1st vector). Z1 (z coordinate 1st vector). X2 (x coordinate 2nd vector). Y2 (y coordinate 2nd vector). Z2 (z coordinate 2nd vector).

Variables altered: None.

Variables returned: D (dot product).

Equations: $\overline{A} \cdot \overline{B} = X_1 X_2 + Y_1 Y_2 + Z_1 Z_2$

Source:
```
 5 REM COMPUTES DOT PRODUCT
10 LET D = (X1*X2) + (Y1*Y2) + (Z1*Z2)
20 RETURN
```

Test Run For Vector Dot-Product

```
RUN
INPUT VARIABLES:
1,2,3,4,5,6
1,2,3,7,8,9
1,2,3,12,11,10
1,2,3,10,11,12
4,5,6,7,8,9
4,5,6,10,11,12
```

RESULTS OF SUBROUTINE:
OUTPUT
32
50
64
68
122
167
RUN TERMINATED
END*

VECTOR ADDITION

Purpose: Finds the sum of two vectors.

Variables needed: X1 (x coordinate of 1st vector). X2 (y coordinate of 2nd vector). Y1 (y coordinate of 1st vector). Y2 (y coordinate of 2nd vector). Z1 (z coordinate of 1st vector). Z2 (z coordinate of 2nd vector).

Variables altered: None.

Variables returned: X3 (x coordinate of new vector). Y3 (y coordinate of new vector). Z3 (z coordinate of new vector).

Equations: $\overline{A} + \overline{B} = X_1 + X_2, \ Y_1 + Y_2, \ Z_1 + Z_2$

Source:
```
 5 REM COMPUTES VECTOR ADDITION
10 LET X3 = X1 + X2
20 LET Y3 = Y1 + Y2
30 LET Z3 = Z1 + Z2
40 RETURN
```

Test Run For Vector Addition
```
RUN
INPUT VARIABLES
1,2,3,4,5,6
1,2,3,7,8,9
1,2,3,12,11,10
1,2,3,10,11,12
4,5,6,7,8,9
4,5,6,10,11,12
RESULTS OF SUBROUTINE:
OUTPUT
5,7,9
8,10,12
13,13,13
11,13,15
11,13,15
14,16,18
RUN TERMINATED
END*
```

VECTOR SUBTRACTION

Purpose: Used to find the difference between two vectors.

Variables needed: X1 (x coordinate of 1st vector). X2 (x coordinate of 2nd vector). Y1 (y coordinate of 1st vector). Y2 (y coordinate of 2nd vector). Z1 (z coordinate of 1st vector). Z2 (z coordinate of 2nd vector).

Variables altered: None.

Variables returned: X3 (x coordinate of new vector). Y3 (y coordinate of new vector). Z3 (z coordinate of new vector).

Equations: $\overline{A}-\overline{B} = X_1-X_2,\ Y_1-Y_2,\ Z_1-Z_2$

Source:

```
 5 REM COMPUTES VECTOR SUBTRACTION
10 LET X3 = X1-X2
20 LET Y3 = Y1-Y2
30 LET Z3 = Z1-Z2
40 RETURN
```

Test Run For Vector Subtraction

```
RUN
INPUT VARIABLES:
1,2,3,4,5,6
1,2,3,7,8,9
1,2,3,12,11,10
4,5,6,7,8,9
RESULTS OF SUBROUTINE:
OUTPUT
-3,-3,-3
-6,-6,-6
-11,-9,-7
-3,-3,-3
RUN TERMINATED
END*
```

Chapter 17
Programming Examples . . . Using
Subroutines and Inline-Substitution

ACCELERATION

```
10 REM THIS PROGRAM COMPUTES THE ACCELERATION
20 REM THE AVERAGE SPEED, THE SPEED AT
30 REM THE END OF THE RUN AND THE
40 REM DISTANCE TRAVELLED AFTER HALF THE TIME
50 REM PERIOD
60 GOSUB 220
70 GOSUB 270
80 GOSUB 290
90 GOSUB 310
100 GOSUB 330
110 PRINT "THE ACCELERATION IS";A
120 PRINT "THE AVERAGE SPEED IS";S
130 PRINT "THE SPEED AFTER ";T;" SECONDS IS";V
140 PRINT "THE DISTANCE TRAVELLED AFTER";S1; "SECONDS IS";D1
150 PRINT
160 PRINT "FOR NEXT RUN TYPE 1, TO STOP TYPE 0"
170 INPUT C
180 IF C=1 THEN 200
190 STOP
200 PRINT
210 GOTO 60
220 PRINT "ENTER DISTANCE TO TRAVEL OVER"
230 INPUT D
235 RETURN
240 PRINT "TIME REQUIRED TO TRAVEL DISTANCE"
250 INPUT T
260 RETURN
270 LET A=(2*D)/T*T
280 RETURN
290 LET S=D/T
300 RETURN
```

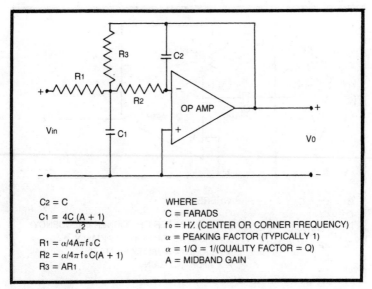

$C_2 = C$

$C_1 = \dfrac{4C(A+1)}{\alpha^2}$

$R_1 = \alpha/4A\pi f_0 C$

$R_2 = \alpha/4\pi f_0 C(A+1)$

$R_3 = AR_1$

WHERE
C = FARADS
f_0 = HZ (CENTER OR CORNER FREQUENCY)
α = PEAKING FACTOR (TYPICALLY 1)
α = 1/Q = 1/(QUALITY FACTOR = Q)
A = MIDBAND GAIN

Fig. 17-1. Low pass filter.

```
310 LET V=A*T
320 RETURN
330 LET S1=T/2
340 LET D1=(A*S1*S1)/2
350 RETURN
360 END
```

ACTIVE FILTERS

These programs allow you to design your own active filters. Schematics for a low pass filter, high pass filter and band pass filter are given in Fig. 17-1, Fig. 17-2 and Fig. 17-3. If you are interested in audio circuits or electronics in general, this programming example can prove very useful. Active filters differ from passive filters in that:

—Active filters contain operational amplifiers.

—Active filters can have gain (higher output than input).

—Active filters have a greater frequency range for a given capacitive-value.

—Active filters need no inductors.

—Active filters need external power supplies.

—Active filters don't have the voltage range of passive devices.

—Active filters always have some nonlinearity.

ACTIVE FILTER DESIGN

```
10 REM THIS PROGRAM COMPUTES HIGH, LOW, AND
20 REM BAND PASS ELEMENTS FROM THE FOLLOWING
```

155

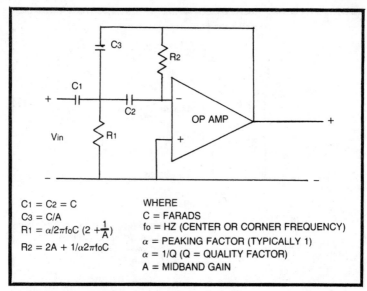

$C_1 = C_2 = C$
$C_3 = C/A$
$R_1 = \alpha/2\pi f_o C (2 + \frac{1}{A})$
$R_2 = 2A + 1/\alpha 2\pi f_o C$

WHERE
C = FARADS
f_o = HZ (CENTER OR CORNER FREQUENCY)
α = PEAKING FACTOR (TYPICALLY 1)
$\alpha = 1/Q$ (Q = QUALITY FACTOR)
A = MIDBAND GAIN

Fig. 17-2. High pass filter.

```
30 REM FREQUENCY, MIDBAND GAIN, A CAPACITOR
40 REM VALUE, AND THE PEAKING FACTOR
50 PRINT"TYPE IN FILTER OPTION:"
60 PRINT"LOW PASS FILTER (LP)"
70 PRINT"HIGH PASS FILTER (HP)"
80 PRINT"BANDPASS FILTER (BP)"
90 INPUT L$
```

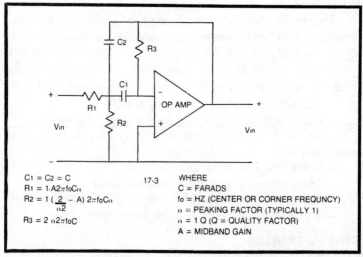

$C_1 = C_2 = C$
$R_1 = 1/A2\pi f_o C\alpha$
$R_2 = 1 (\frac{2}{\alpha^2} - A) 2\pi f_o C\alpha$
$R_3 = 2 \alpha 2\pi f_o C$

17-3

WHERE
C = FARADS
f_o = HZ (CENTER OR CORNER FREQUENCY)
α = PEAKING FACTOR (TYPICALLY 1)
$\alpha = 1/Q$ (Q = QUALITY FACTOR)
A = MIDBAND GAIN

Fig. 17-3. Band pass filter.

```
100 IF L$="LP" THEN 150
110 IF L$="HP" THEN 280
120 IF L$="BP" THEN 410
130 PRINT"INVALID RESPONSE"
140 GOTO 50
150 GOSUB 540
160 LET C2=C
170 LET C1=(4*C*(A+1))/B*B
180 LET R1=P/(4*A*P*F*C)
190 LET R2=P/(4*P*F*C*(A+1))
200 LET R3=A*R1
210 PRINT"COMPONENTS OF LOW PASS FILTER"
220 PRINT"RESISTOR R1=";R1
230 PRINT"RESISTOR R2=";R2
240 PRINT"RESISTOR R3=";R3
250 PRINT"CAPACITOR C1=";C1
260 PRINT"CAPACITOR C2=";C2
270 GOTO 660
280 GOSUB 540
290 LET C1=C
300 LET C2=C
310 LET C3=C/A
320 LET R1=B/((2*P*F*C)*(2+(1/A)))
330 LET R2 = ((¼*A)+1/(B*2*P*F*C)
340 PRINT"COMPONENTS OF HIGH PASS FILTER"
350 PRINT"RESISTOR R1=";R1
360 PRINT"RESISTOR R2=";R2
370 PRINT"CAPACITOR C1=";C1
380 PRINT"CAPACITOR C2=";C2
390 PRINT"CAPACITOR C3=";C3
400 GOTO 660
410 GOSUB 540
420 LET C1 C
430 LET C2 C
440 LET R1=1/(A*2*P*F*C*B)
450 LET R2=1/(((2/B*B)-A)*2*P*F*C*B)
460 LET R3=2/(B*2*P*F*C)
470 PRINT"COMPONENTS OF BANDPASS FILTER"
480 PRINT"RESISTOR R1=";R1
490 PRINT"RESISTOR R2=";R2
500 PRINT "RESISTOR R3=";R3
510 PRINT"CAPACITOR C1=";C1
520 PRINT"CAPACITOR C2=";C2
530 GOTO 660
540 PRINT
550 PRINT"ENTER FREQUENCY F(HZ)"
560 INPUT F
570 PRINT"ENTER CAPACITOR C(F)"
580 INPUT C
590 PRINT"ENTER PEAKING FACTOR"
600 INPUT B
610 PRINT"ENTER MIDBAND GAIN"
620 INPUT A
630 LET P=3.14159
640 PRINT
650 RETURN
```

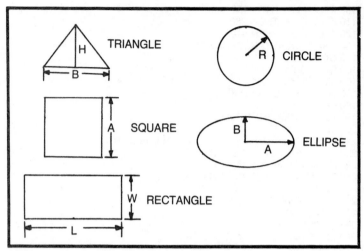

Fig. 17-4. Areas of geometric plane figures.

```
660 PRINT
670 PRINT"TO COMPUTE NEXT FILTER COMPONENTS"
680 PRINT"TYPE NEXT, IF NOT TYPE STOP"
690 INPUT L$
700 IF L$="NEXT" THEN 740
710 IF L$="STOP" THEN 760
720 PRINT"INVALID COMMAND"
730 GOTO 670
740 PRINT
750 GOTO 50
760 END
```

AREAS OF GEOMETRIC PLANE FIGURES

Figure 17-4 illustrates geometric plane figures.

```
10 REM THIS PROGRAM COMPUTES AREA
20 PRINT "TYPE 1 FOR LIST OF OPTIONS, 0 TO START"
30 INPUT C
40 IF C=0 THEN 110
50 PRINT "OPTIONS ARE AS FOLLOWS:"
60 PRINT "(1) CIRCLE"
70 PRINT "(2) ELLIPSE"
80 PRINT "(3) TRIANGLE"
90 PRINT "(4) SQUARE"
100 PRINT "(5) RECTANGLE"
110 PRINT "ENTER NUMBER REPRESENTING THE FIGURE DESIRED"
120 INPUT C
130 ON C GOSUB 150,190,230,270,310
140 PRINT "THE AREA IS ";X
145 GOTO 350
150 PRINT "RADIUS"
160 INPUT R
170 LET X=3.14159*R*R
```

```
180 RETURN
190 PRINT "ENTER MINOR AND MAJOR AXES"
200 INPUT B,A
210 LET X=3.14159*A*B
220 RETURN
230 PRINT "HEIGHT AND BASE"
240 INPUT A,B
250 LET X=A*B/2
260 RETURN
270 PRINT "ENTER SIDE"
280 INPUT A
290 LET X=A*A
300 RETURN
310 PRINT "WIDTH AND LENGTH"
320 INPUT W,L
330 LET X=L*W
340 RETURN
350 PRINT "FOR NEXT RUN TYPE 1, TO STOP TYPE 0"
360 INPUT C
370 IF C=1 THEN 390
380 STOP
390 PRINT
400 GOTO 20
410 END
```

CENTRIPETAL FORCE

```
10 REM THIS PROGRAM COMPUTES THE CENTRIPETAL FORCE
20 REM AND THE CENTRIPETAL ACCELERATION
30 PRINT "ENTER THE MASS OF THE OBJECT IN KILOGRAMS"
40 INPUT M
50 PRINT "ENTER THE LINEAR SPEED IN METERS/SECOND"
60 INPUT V
70 PRINT "ENTER THE RADIUS OF THE CIRCLE THE OBJECT IS MOVING
IN"
80 INPUT R
90 GOSUB 190
100 GOSUB 210
110 PRINT "THE CENTRIPETAL FORCE IS ";F;" NEWTONS"
120 PRINT "THE CENTRIPETAL ACCELERATION IS ";A;" METERS/
SECOND/SECOND"
130 PRINT
135 PRINT "TO CONTINUE TYPE 1, TO STOP TYPE 0"
140 INPUT C
150 IF C=1 THEN 170
160 STOP
170 PRINT
180 GOTO 30
190 LET F=(M*V*V)/R
200 RETURN
210 LET A=V*V/R
220 RETURN
230 END
```

CONSERVATION OF MOMENTUM

The conservation of momentum formula (vector relationship) is: $M_1V_1 + M_2V_2 = (M_1+M_2)V_f$

159

```
10 REM IF TWO BODIES (OBJECTS) COLLIDE AT
11 REM RIGHT ANGLES TO EACH OTHER AND
20 REM STICK TOGETHER, THIS COLLISION
30 REM IS CALLED COMPLETELY INELASTIC
40 REM THIS PROGRAM COMPUTES THE DIRECTION
41 REM AFTER THE IMPACT AND
50 REM THE RESULTING NEW SPEED OF THE
55 REM COMPOSITE OBJECT
60 PRINT "ENTER THE MASS OF THE FIRST OBJECT"
70 INPUT M1
80 PRINT "ENTER THE MASS OF THE SECOND OBJECT"
90 INPUT M2
100 PRINT "ENTER THE SPEED OF THE FIRST OBJECT"
110 INPUT V1
120 PRINT "ENTER THE SPEED OF THE SECOND OBJECT"
130 INPUT V2
140 GOSUB 230
145 PRINT "THE DIRECTION IS ";D;" DEGREES"
150 PRINT "THE RESULTING NEW SPEED IS ";V
160 PRINT
170 PRINT "TO CONTINUE TYPE 1, IF NOT TYPE 0"
180 INPUT C
190 IF C=1 THEN 210
200 STOP
210 PRINT
220 GOTO 60
230 LET J=(M1*V1)/(M1+Ms)
240 LET L=(M2*V2)/(M1+M2)
250 LET V=SQR(J*J+L*L)
```

DENSITY

```
10 REM THIS PROGRAM COMPUTES THE MASS OF A VOLUME,
20 REM THE NUMBER OF ATOMS IN THAT VOLUME
30 REM THE MASS OF 1 ATOM OF THAT ELEMENT
40 REM AND THE AVERAGE VOLUME OF THE ATOMS OF THAT ELEMENT
50 PRINT "ENTER DENSITY OF THE ELEMENT"
60 INPUT D
70 PRINT "ENTER THE VOLUME OF THE SUBSTANCE"
80 INPUT V
84 PRINT "ENTER THE ATOMIC WEIGHT OF THAT ELEMENT"
85 INPUT W
90 GOSUB 210
100 PRINT "THE MASS OF THE VOLUME IS ";M
110 PRINT "THE NUMBER OF ATOMS ARE ";A
120 PRINT "THE MASS OF ONE ATOM IS ";M1
130 PRINT "THE AVERAGE VOLUME IS ";V1
140 PRINT
150 PRINT "TO CONTINUE TYPE 1, TO STOP TYPE 0"
160 INPUT C
170 IF C=1 THEN 190
180 STOP
190 PRINT
200 GOTO 50
210 LET M=D*V
220 LET A=(M*6.02217E23)/W
230 LET M1=M/A
240 LET V1=V/A
```

```
250 RETURN
260 END
300 INPUT M
310 PRINT "WHAT IS THE DISTANCE TO FALL THRU IN METERS"
320 INPUT D
330 LET T=(−M+SQR(M*M−19.62*D))/9.81
340 LET T1=(−M−SQR(M*M−19.62*D))/9.81
350 IF T>=0 THEN 370
360 LET T1=T
370 RETURN
380 END
```

ENERGY

```
10 REM THIS PROGRAM COMPUTES ENERGY IN JOULES AND
20 REM ALSO IN ELECTRON VOLTS
30 PRINT "ENTER THE MASS IN KILOGRAMS"
40 INPUT K
45 GOSUB 160
50 GOSUB 180
60 PRINT "THE ENERGY EQUIVALENT OF ";K;" KILOGRAMS"
70 PRINT "IS ";E;" JOULES"
80 PRINT "WHICH IS THE SAME AS ";V;" ELECTRON VOLTS"
90 PRINT
100 PRINT "TO CONTINUE TYPE 1, TO STOP TYPE 0"
110 INPUT C
120 IF C=1 THEN 140
130 STOP
140 PRINT
150 GOTO 30
160 LET E=K*8.9874E16
170 RETURN
180 LET V=E/1.6022E-19
190 RETURN
200 END
```

FORCE

In Fig. 17-5, Y components cancel because $\Theta = \Theta 2$

```
10 REM THIS PROGRAM ASSUMES THAT THE FORCE IS
20 REM APPLIED BY A ROPE OR WIRE (ETC) FROM
30 REM TWO OBJECTS FURNISHING THE FORCES AND
40 REM THEY ARE MOVING IN THE SAME DIRECTION
50 PRINT "ENTER FORCE ONE IN NEWTONS"
51 INPUT F1
52 PRINT "ENTER FORCE TWO IN NEWTONS"
60 INPUT F2
70 PRINT "WHAT IS THE COMMON DISTANCE"
80 PRINT "FROM THE FORCE SUPPLYING OBJECT TO THE OBJECT WHICH"
81 PRINT "IS THE POINT OF FORCE"
82 PRINT "THIS DISTANCE iS IN METERS"
90 INPUT M
100 PRINT "WHAT IS THE SEPARATION OF THE TWO FORCES IN METERS"
```

161

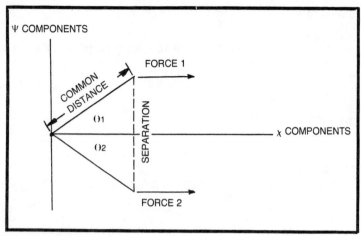

Fig. 17-5. Force.

```
110 INPUT M1
120 GOSUB 200
130 PRINT "THE TOTAL APPLIED FORCE IS ";F;" NEWTONS"
140 PRINT
141 PRINT "TO CONTINUE TYPE 1, TO STOP TYPE 0"
150 INPUT C
160 IF C=1 THEN 180
170 STOP
180 PRINT
190 GOTO 50
200 LET T=ASIN((M1/2)/(M))
210 LET X=F1*COS(T)
220 LET X1=F2*COS(T)
230 LET F=X+X1
240 RETURN
250 END
```

FREE FALL

```
10 REM THIS PROGRAM COMPUTES THE TIME REQUIRED
20 REM FOR AN OBJECT TO FALL THRU X
30 REM DISTANCE AND IT MAY HAVE AN INITIAL
40 REM VELOCITY
50 PRINT "IS DISTANCE IN METERS (1) OR IN FEET (0)"
60 INPUT C
70 IF C=1 THEN 180
80 GOSUB 200
100 PRINT "TIME REQUIRED IS ";T;" SECONDS"
110 PRINT
120 PRINT "TO CONTINUE TYPE 1, TO STOP TYPE 0"
130 INPUT C
140 IF C= 1 THEN 160
150 STOP
160 PRINT
```

```
170 GOTO 50
180 GOSUB 290
190 GOTO 100
200 PRINT "WHAT IS THE INITIAL VELOCITY IN FEET"
210 INPUT F
220 PRINT "WHAT IS THE DISTANCE TO FALL THRU IN FEET"
230 INPUT D
240 LET T = (−F+SQR(F*F−64.4*D))/32.2
250 LET T=(−F−SQR(F*F−64.4*D))/32.2
260 IF T>=0 THEN 280
270 LET T1=T
280 RETURN
290 PRINT "WHAT IS THE INITIAL VELOCITY IN METERS"
```

FRESNEL INTEGRALS

Fresnel integrals are often used in such varied subjects as:

—Orbital mechanics—would you like to write that super rocket game.

—Acoustics—calculating how much a barrier reduces the sound or noise level.

—Number theory.

—Fresnel diffraction and fresnel lenses.

The following example computes the two integrals C(Z) and S(Z) and is in integral notation:

$$C(Z)=\int_0^2 COS(\pi + {}^2/2)dt$$
$$S(Z)=\int_0^2 SIN(\pi + {}^2/2)dt$$

These two equations can be solved directly in terms of sines and cosines:

$$C(Z)=\tfrac{1}{2}+f(Z)\ SIN(\pi Z^2/2)-g(Z)COS(\pi Z^2/2)$$
$$S(Z)=\tfrac{1}{2}-f(Z)COS(\pi Z^2/2)-g(Z)SIN(\pi Z^2/2)$$

where

$$f(Z)=(1+0.926Z)/2+1.792Z+3.104Z^2$$

and

$$g(Z)=\tfrac{1}{2}+4.142Z+3.49Z^2+6.67Z^3$$

approximate error is less than 2.0×10^{-3}

```
10 REM THIS PROGRAM COMPUTES FRESNEL INTEGRALS
20 LET P=3.14159
30 PRINT "WHICH INTEGRAL DO YOU WISH TO EVALUATE"
40 PRINT "C(Z) OR S(Z), TYPE EITHER C OR S"
50 INPUT L$
60 PRINT "ENTER THE VALUE OF Z"
70 INPUT Z
80 IF L$="C" THEN 120
90 IF L$="S" THEN 190
100 PRINT "INVALID RESPONSE TO CHOICE OF INTEGRAL"
110 GOTO 30
```

```
120 GOSUB 270
130 GOSUB 320
140 GOSUB 360
150 LET C=(0.5)+(A*SIN(D))−(B*COS(D))
160 PRINT
170 PRINT "C(";Z;") ";C
180 GOTO 380
190 GOSUB 270
200 GOSUB 320
210 GOSUB 360
220 LET S=(0.5)−(A*COS(D))−(B*SIN(D))
230 PRINT
240 PRINT"S(";Z;") ";S
250 GOTO 380
260 REM (A) SUBROUTINE
270 LET A=(1+(0.926*Z))
280 LET E=(2+(1.792*Z))+(3.104*Z ↑ 2)
290 LET A=A/E
300 RETURN
310 REM (B) SUBROUTINE
320 LET E=(2+(4.142*Z))+(3.492*Z ↑2)+(6.67*Z ↑ 3)
330 LET B=1/E
340 RETURN
350 REM (D) SUBROUTINE
360 LET D=(P*Z ↑ 2)/2
370 RETURN
380 PRINT
390 PRINT "TO CONTINUE TYPE Y, IF NOT TYPE N"
400 INPUT X$
410 IF X$="Y" THEN 440
420 PRINT "FRESNEL SAYS GOOD-BYE"
430 STOP
440 PRINT
450 GOTO 30
460 END
```

GAS LAWS

The Gas Laws formula is: $\dfrac{P_1}{T_1} = \dfrac{P_2}{T_2}$

where T_1 and T_2 are in *k

```
10 REM THIS PROGRAM COMPUTES THE GAS LAWS
20 REM THIS PROGRAM ALSO ASSUMES THE CONTAINER
30 REM OF THE GAS IS A FLEXIBLE BALLOON TYPE
40 REM OF DEVICE
50 PRINT "ENTER INITIAL PRESSURE IN N/CM2"
60 INPUT P1
70 PRINT "ENTER TEMPERATURE IN DEGREES KELVIN AT INITIAL TIME"
80 INPUT T1
100 PRINT "ENTER FINAL TEMPERATURE IN DEGREES KELVIN"
110 INPUT T2
115 GOSUB 200
120 PRINT "FINAL PRESSURE IS "P;" N/CM2"
130 PRINT
140 PRINT "TO CONTINUE TYPE 1, IF NOT TYPE 0"
150 INPUT C
```

```
160 IF C=1 THEN 180
170 STOP
180 PRINT
190 GOTO 50
200 REM SUBROUTINE
210 LET P=(P1*T2)/T1
220 RETURN
230 END
```

GRAVITATION

This program computes gravitation as illustrated in Fig. 17-6.

```
10 REM THIS PROGRAM COMPUTES THE LINEAR VELOCITY
20 REM RELATIVE TO THE PRIMARY AND THE ACCELERATION
30 REM DUE TO GRAVITY
40 PRINT "ENTER DISTANCE FROM PRIMARY TO SECONDARY"
50 INPUT R
60 PRINT "ENTER THE MASS OF THE PRIMARY IN KILOGRAMS"
70 INPUT K
80 GOSUB 190
90 GOSUB 210
100 PRINT "THE ACCELERATION DUE TO GRAVITY IS ";G
110 PRINT "THE LINEAR VELOCITY OF THE SECONDARY IS ";S
120 PRINT
130 PRINT "TO CONTINUE TYPE 1, IF NOT TYPE 0 TO STOP"
140 INPUT C
150 IF C=1 THEN 170
160 STOP
170 PRINT
180 GOTO 40
190 LET G=(6.6732E—11*K)/(R*R)
200 RETURN
210 LET S=SQR (G*R)
220 RETURN
230 END
260 LET D=ATAN(L/J)
270 RETURN
280 END
```

HYPERBOLA

A hyperbola is a member of the family of curves called conic sections. It is the line drawn by a point that moves in such a way that the difference of its distance from two other points remains constant. The standard formula for a hyperbola is:

$$X^2/A^2 - Y^2/B^2 = 1$$

The polar equation is given as:

$$r = \frac{a(e^2-1)}{(e\cos\Theta - 1)}$$

The hyperbola, parabola, circle and ellipse are all members of the family of conic sections which are formed by slicing a cone at different angles.

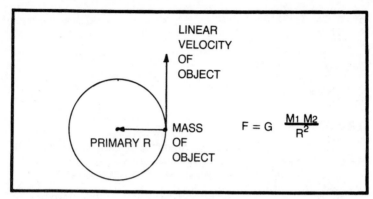

Fig. 17-6. Gravitation.

HYPERBOLIC AND INVERSE HYPERBOLIC
FUNCTIONS (in-line substitution example)

```
10 REM THIS PROGRAM COMPUTES HYPERBOLIC FUNCTIONS
20 REM AND THEIR INVERSES. IT IS ASSUMED
30 REM THAT THE (BASIC) FUNCTION LOG IS BASE E
40 PRINT "FOR INSTRUCTIONS TYPE"
50 PRINT "EITHER YES OR NO"
60 INPUT L$
70 IF L$="YES" THEN 110
80 IF L$="NO" THEN 190
90 PRINT "INVALID COMMAND"
100 GOTO 40
110 PRINT "HYPERBOLIC AND INVERSE HYPERBOLIC FUNCTIONS"
120 PRINT "TYPE IN FUNCTION NAME THEN THE ARGUMENT WITH"
130 PRINT "A COMMA BETWEEN THEM."
140 PRINT "FOR EXAMPLE- SINH(X), WHERE X=4"
150 PRINT "WOULD BE ENTERED AS SINH,4"
160 PRINT "AVAILABLE FUNCTIONS ARE- SINH, COSH, TANH,"
170 PRINT "CSCH, SECH, COTH, ASINH, ACOSH, ATANH, ACSCH,"
180 PRINT "ASECH AND ACOTH."
190 PRINT
200 PRINT "FUNCTION"
210 INPUT F$,X
220 IF F$="SINH" THEN 360
230 IF F$="COSH" THEN 380
240 IF F$="TANH" THEN 400
250 IF F$="CSCH" THEN 420
260 IF F$="SECH" THEN 440
270 IF F$="COTH" THEN 460
280 IF F$="ASINH" THEN 480
290 IF F$="ACOSH" THEN 500
300 IF F$="ATANH" THEN 520
310 IF F$="ACSCH" THEN 540
320 IF F$="ASECH" THEN 560
330 IF F$="ACOTH" THEN 580
340 PRINT "INVALID COMMAND"
350 GOTO 200
```

```
360 LET Z=(EXP(X)-EXP(-X))/2
370 GOTO 590
380 LET Z=(EXP(X)+EXP(-X))/2
390 GOTO 590
400 LET Z=(EXP(X)-EXP(-X))/(EXP(X)+EXP(-X))
410 GOTO 590
420 LET Z=1/((EXP(X)-EXP(-X))/2)
430 GOTO 590
440 LET Z=1/((EXP(X)+EXP(-X))/2)
450 GOTO 590
460 LET Z=1/((EXP(X)-EXP(-X))/(EXP(X)+EXP(-X)))
470 GOTO 590
480 LET Z=LOG(X+SQR((X*X) 1))
490 GOTO 590
500 LET Z=LOG(X+SQR((X*X)-1))
510 GOTO 590
520 LET Z=(LOG((1+X)/(1-X)))/2
530 GOTO 590
540 LET Z=(EXP(1/X)-EXP(-1/X))/2
550 GOTO 590
560 LET Z=(EXP(1/X)+EXP(-1/X))/2
570 GOTO 590
580 LET Z=(EXP(1/X)-EXP(-1/X))/(EXP(1/X)+EXP(-1/X))
590 PRINT
600 PRINT F$;"(;X;")= ";Z
610 PRINT
620 PRINT "FOR NEXT FUNCTION TYPE YES, IF NOT TYPE NO"
630 INPUT L$
640 IF L$="YES" THEN 660
650 STOP
660 PRINT
670 GOTO 40
680 END
```

MAGIC SQUARES

A magic square is a square matrix of numbers such that the numbers in either diagonal or any row or column add up to the same value. Figure 17-7 is an example of a magic square.

8	1	6
3	5	7
4	9	2

Any column or row or either diagonal adds up to 15. This program allows you to "play" against the computer in the creation of the magic square.

```
1 REM MAGIC SQUARES (1977)
2 PRINT"MAGIC SQUARES"
3 PRINT
4 PRINT"ARE INSTRUCTIONS REQUIRED (TYPE 1 FOR YES, 0 FOR NO)"
5 INPUT T : IF T=1 THEN 10
6 GOTO 82
10 PRINT "YOU ARE TRYING TO CREATE A MAGIC SQUARE"
```

167

Fig. 17-7. A magic square.

```
20 PRINT "A MAGIC SQUARE IS A SQUARE ARRAY OF"
25 PRINT "NUMBERS SUCH THAT IF YOU ADD UP THE"
30 PRINT "DIAGONALS, ROWS OR COLUMNS YOU ARRIVE"
40 PRINT "AT THE SAME SUM!!"
45 PRINT "THE COMPUTER IS TRYING TO BLOCK YOU IN"
46 PRINT "SUCH A FASHION AS THAT YOU WILL CREATE"
47 PRINT "A COLUMN, ROW OR DIAGONAL THAT DOES NOT"
50 PRINT "ADD UP TO 15 AS IS NECESSARY IN THIS CASE."
60 PRINT "TO WIN YOU MUST FORCE THE COMPUTER"
65 PRINT "TO CREATE A WRONG SUM!!!"
70 PRINT "IN THE CASE OF A MAGIC SQUARE BEING"
75 PRINT "CREATED.......IT IS A TIE GAME!
80 PRINT
81 PRINT "GOOD-LUCK—TYPE ANY NUMBER TO START" : INPUT T
82 PRINT
83 DIM A(10), B(10)
84 PRINT : PRINT
85 PRINT "HERE ARE THE CELL NUMBERS" : PRINT
90 PRINT "1", "2", "3" : PRINT
91 PRINT "4", "5", "6" : PRINT
92 PRINT "7", "8", "9"
95 FOR I=1 TO 9
96 A(I)=0 : B(I)=0
97 NEXT I
98 M=0 : W=0
100 PRINT : INPUT "YOUR MOVE—CELL, NUMBER",I,N
105 IF I<1 OR I>9 OR N<1 OR N>9 THEN 130
110 IF A(I)=0 AND B(N)=0 THEN 150
130 PRINT : PRINT "ILLEGAL MOVE" : GOTO 100
150 A(I)=N : B(N)=1 : M=M+1
170 GOSUB 960
180 GOSUB 800
200 IF W=0 THEN 230
210 PRINT "SORRY, YOU LOSE—NICE TRY" : GOTO 560
230 IF M<5 THEN 400
240 PRINT "A TIE GAME !!" : GOTO 560
400 FOR Q=1 TO 9
410 IF A(Q)>0 THEN 470
420 FOR R=1 TO 9
430 IF B(R)>0 THEN 470
435 A(Q)=R
440 GOSUB 800
450 IF W=0 THEN 500
460 Q1=Q : R1=R : W=0 : A(Q)=0
```

```
470 NEXT R
480 NEXT Q
490 W=1 : R=R1 : W=0 : A(Q)=0
500 B(R)=1
520 PRINT : PRINT "THE COMPUTER MOVES TO CELL ";Q
521 PRINT "WITH A ";R
530 GOSUB 960
540 IF W=0 THEN 100
550 PRINT : PRINT "THE COMPUTER LOSES!!!"
560 PRINT : PRINT "LETS TRY AGAIN" : GOTO 84
800 FOR X=1 TO 8
810 GOTO (X*10+810)
820 J=1 : K=2 : L=2 : GOTO 900
830 K=4 : L=7 : GOTO 900
840 K=5 : L=9 : GOTO 900
850 J=4 : L=6 : GOTO 900
860 J=2 : L=8 : GOTO 900
870 J=3 : L=7 : GOTO 900
880 K=6 : L=9 : GOTO 900
890 J=7 : K=8 : GOTO 900
900 IF A(J)=0 OR A(K)=0 OR A(L)=0 THEN 930
920 IF A(J)+A(K)+A(L)<>15 THEN 940
930 NEXT X
935 GOTO 950
940 W=1
950 RETURN
960 PRINT : PRINT A(1), A(2), A(3)
961 PRINT
970 PRINT A(4), A(5), A(6)
971 PRINT
980 PRINT A(7), A(8), A(9)
990 RETURN
999 END
```

MOLES

The formulas for moles are:

$$\text{moles} = \frac{\text{mass}}{\text{atomic weight(s)}}$$

$$\text{molecules} = \text{moles} \times \text{Avogadro's number}$$
$$\text{volume (stp)} = 22.414 \times \text{moles}$$

where Avogadro's number is 6.02217×10^{23}

```
10 REM THIS PROGRAM COMPUTES THE NUMBER OF MOLES,
20 REM THE NUMBER OF MOLECULES IN X GRAMS OF A
30 REM SUBSTANCE (GAS)
35 REM THIS PROGRAM ALSO COMPUTES THE VOLUME AT STP
40 PRINT "ENTER THE NUMBER OF GRAMS"
41 PRINT "OF THE DESIRED SUBSTANCE (GAS)"
50 INPUT G
60 PRINT "ENTER THE ATOMIC WEIGHT OF THE GAS"
70 INPUT W
```

```
80 GOSUB 190
90 PRINT "THE NUMBER OF MOLES IS ";M
100 PRINT "THE NUMBER OF MOLECULES IS ";A
110 PRINT "THE VOLUME AT STP IS ";V;" LITERS"
120 PRINT
130 PRINT "TO CONTINUE TYPE 1, IF NOT TYPE 0"
140 INPUT C
150 IF C = 1 THEN 170
160 STOP
170 PRINT
180 GOTO 40
190 LET M = G/W
200 LET A = M*6.02217E23
210 LET V = M*22.414
220 RETURN
230 END
```

PARALLEL IMPEDANCES

Impedance is the "equivalent" in AC circuits of resistance in DC circuits. It is, however, more complex than simple voltage and resistance.

The formula is: $I=V/Z$ where Z is a complex number made up of resistance (the real part) and reactance (the imaginary part).

In the polar form of complex numbers, the angle obtained is actually present in the circuit—even though it is called imaginary. See Fig. 17-8 for the types of parallel impedances and Fig. 17-9 for the types of series impedances.

```
10 REM THIS PROGRAM COMPUTES THE IMPEDANCE OF THE
20 REM FOLLOWING PARALLEL CIRCUITS R/L, R/C
30 REM L/C, R/L/C, RL/C, LR/CR
40 REM IT IS ASSUMED THAT ALL TRIG FUNCTIONS ARE
50 REM OPERATED IN THE RADIAN MODE
60 PRINT "TYPES AVAILABLE ARE R/L(1), R/C(2)"
70 PRINT "L/C(3), R/L/C(4), RL/C(5) AND LR/CR(6)"
80 PRINT "TYPE THE NUMBER THAT REPRESENTS THE CIRCUIT"
90 INPUT X
100 ON X GOTO 110, 190, 270, 410, 510, 610
120 PRINT "R(OHMS), L(HENRIES), AND F(HERTZ)"
130 INPUT R,L,F
140 GOSUB 840
150 LET Z=R*R1/SQR(R*R+R1*R1)
160 LET P=ATN(R/R1)
170 GOSUB 880
180 GOTO 730
190 GOSUB 820
200 PRINT "R(OHMS), C(MFD) AND F(HERTZ)"
210 INPUT R,C,F
220 GOSUB 860
230 LET Z=R*R2/SQR(R*R+R2*R2)
240 LET P=ATN(—R/R2)
250 GOSUB 880
260 GOTO 730
```

170

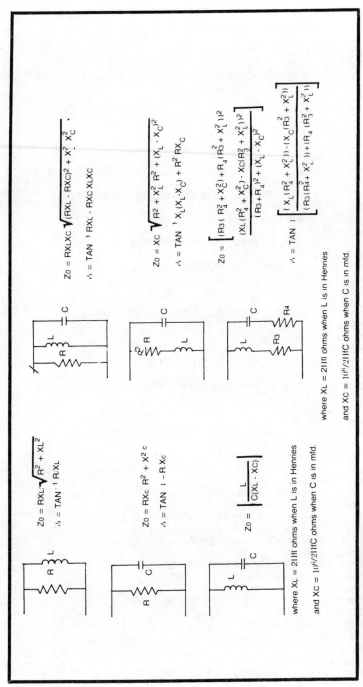

Fig. 17-8. Parallel impedances.

```
270 GOSUB 820
280 PRINT"L(HENRIES), C(MFD), F(HERTZ)"
290 INPUT L,C,F
300 GOSUB 840
310 GOSUB 860
320 LET Z=ABS (L/(C*R1—R2))
330 IF R1=R2 THEN 370
340 IF R1>R2 THEN 390
350 LET P=90
360 GOTO 730
370 LET P=0
380 GOTO 730
390 LET P=—90
400 GOTO 730
410 GOSUB 820
420 PRINT "R(OHMS), C(MFD), L(HENRIES) AND F(HERTZ)
430 INPUT R,C,L,F
440 GOSUB 840
450 GOSUB 860
460 LET Z=((R*R1)—(R*R2))↑2+(R1*R1*R2*R2)
470 LET Z=R*R1*R2/SQR(Z)
480 LET P=ATN(((R*R1)—(R*R2))/(R1*R2))
490 GOSUB 880
500 GOTO 730
510 GOSUB 820
520 PRINT "R(OHMS), L(HENRIES), C(MFD) AND F(HERTZ)"
530 INPUT R,L,C,F
540 GOSUB 840
550 GOSUB 860
560 LET Z=(R*R+R1*R1)/(R*R+(R1—R2)↑2)
570 LET Z=R2*SQR(Z)
580 LET P=ATN((R1*(R1—R2))+(R↑2/(R*R2)))
590 GOSUB 880
600 GOTO 730
610 GOSUB 820
620 PRINT "L(HENRIES), C(MFD), R3(OHMS) AND R4(OHMS)"
630 PRINT"F(HERTZ)"
640 INPUT L,C,R3,R4,F
650 GOSUB 840
660 GOSUB 860
670 LET A=R4*R4+R2*R2
680 LET B=R3*R3+R1*R1
690 LET Z=((R3*A+(R4*B))↑2)+((R1*A—(R2*B))↑2)
700 LET Z=SQR(Z/(((R3+R4)↑2)+((R1—R2)↑2))
71) LET P=ATN(((R1*A)—(R2*B))/((R3*A)+(R4*B)))
720 GOSUB 880
730 PRINT "IMPEDANCE, Z=";Z;" OHMS"
740 PRINT "PHASE ANGLE=";P;" DEGREES
750 PRINT
760 PRINT "TO CONTINUE TYPE Y, IF NOT TYPE N"
770 INPUT Q$
780 IF Q$="Y" THEN 800
790 STOP
800 PRINT
810 GOTO 60
820 PRINT "ENTER CIRCUIT PARAMETERS"
```

```
830 RETURN
840 LET R1=6.28318*F*L
850 RETURN
860 LET R2=1E06/(6.28318*F*C)
870 RETURN
880 LET P=(P*180)/3.14159
890 RETURN
900 END
```

PASCAL'S TRIANGLE

If the coefficients of $(A+B)^k$ in a binomial series are arranged as a series of rows, then as k increases, the shape resembles a triangle:

```
1
1  1
1  2  1
1  3  3  1
1  4  6  4  1
1  5  10  10  5  1
```

Pascal's triangle is useful for statistics and probability theory.

```
10 REM THIS PROGRAM GENERATES THE ELEMENTS IN ANY ROW
20 REM OF A PASCAL TRIANGLE
30 PRINT "ENTER ROW NUMBER"
40 INPUT R
50 LET R=R-1
60 LET R1=R
70 LET N=R1
80 GOSUB 270
90 LET R2=N
100 LET N=R1
110 GOSUB 270
120 LET R3=N
130 LET N=R-R1
140 GOSUB 270
150 LET R4=R2/(N*R3)
160 PRINT R4
170 LET R1=R1-1
180 IF R1<0 THEN 200
190 GOTO 70
200 PRINT "ROW COMPLETE"
210 PRINT "TO CONTINUE TYPE Y, IF NOT TYPE N"
220 INPUT L$
230 IF L$="Y" THEN 250
240 STOP
250 PRINT
260 GOTO 30
270 LET Z=1
280 FOR I=1 TO N
290 LET Z=Z*I
300 NEXT I
310 LET N=Z
320 RETURN
330 END
```

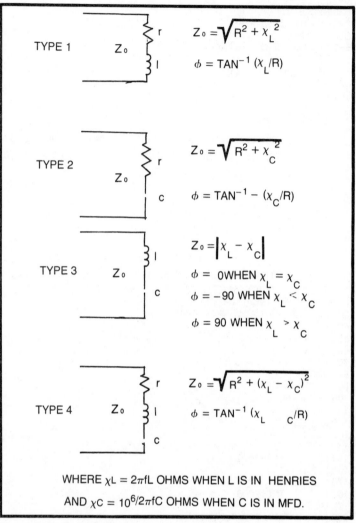

Fig. 17-9. Series, impedances.

RADIOACTIVE HALF LIFE

The formula for radioactive half-life is:

$$N_t = N_0 e^{-kt}$$

where N_0 = number of atoms

N_t = number of atoms left

k = disintegration constant for that element

t = time in seconds

```
10 REM THIS PROGRAM SOLVES USING THE
20 REM DISINTEGRATION CONSTANT OF THE ELEMENT
30 REM FOR HALF-LIFE OF A RADIO-ACTIVE SUBSTANCE
40 PRINT "ENTER THE DISINTEGRATION CONSTANT"
50 INPUT K
60 GOSUB 160
70 PRINT "THE HALF-LIFE IS ";H
80 GOSUB 180
90 PRINT "THE NUMBER OF ATOMS STILL LEFT IS ";L
100 PRINT
105 PRINT "TO CONTINUE TYPE 1, TO STOP TYPE 0"
110 INPUT C
120 IF C= 1 THEN 140
130 STOP
140 PRINT
150 GOTO 40
160 LET H = 0.693/K
170 RETURN
180 PRINT "THE NUMBER OF ATOMS AT STARTING POINT IS"
190 INPUT N
200 PRINT "ENTER THE DESIRED TIME PERIOD IN SECONDS"
210 INPUT S
220 LET L = N*EXP(–K*S)
230 RETURN
240 END
```

SECTIONS

This example demonstrates in-line substitution. See Fig. 17-10.

```
10 REM THE FOLLOWING PROGRAM COMPUTES THE
20 REM VARIOUS PARAMETERS INVOLVED WITH ANNULAR,
30 REM CIRCULAR AND RECTANGULAR SECTIONS
40 PRINT" THE VARIOUS SECTIONS AVAILABLE ARE :—"
50 PRINT"ANNULAR (A)"
60 PRINT"CIRCULAR (C)"
70 PRINT"RECTANGULAR (R)"
80 PRINT"TYPE EITHER A, C OR R"
90 INPUT A$
100 IF A$="A" THEN 150
110 IF A$="C" THEN 230
120 IF A$="R" THEN 320
130 PRINT"INVALID COMMAND"
140 GOTO 40
150 PRINT
160 PRINT"ENTER INSIDE AND OUTSIDE DIAMETERS (D1,D2)"
170 INPUT D1,D2
180 LET P=3.14159
190 LET I=(P*((D2↑4)–(D1↑4)))/64
200 LET J=I*2
210 LET A=(P*((D2*D2)–(D1*D1)))/4
220 GOTO 380
230 PRINT
240 PRINT"ENTER RADIUS"
250 INPUT R
260 LET P=3.14159
```

```
270 LET D=2*R
280 LET I=(P*(D↑4))/64
290 LET J=I*2
300 LET A=(P*(D*D))/4
310 GOTO 380
320 PRINT
330 PRINT"ENTER BASE AND HEIGHT"
340 INPUT B,H
350 LET I=(B*(H*H*H))/12
360 LET J=(B*H*(B*B+H*H))/12
370 LET A=B*H
380 PRINT
390 PRINT"****PARAMETERS****"
```

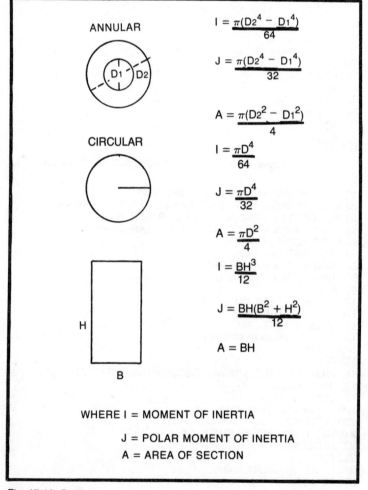

ANNULAR

$$I = \frac{\pi(D_2^4 - D_1^4)}{64}$$

$$J = \frac{\pi(D_2^4 - D_1^4)}{32}$$

$$A = \frac{\pi(D_2^2 - D_1^2)}{4}$$

CIRCULAR

$$I = \frac{\pi D^4}{64}$$

$$J = \frac{\pi D^4}{32}$$

$$A = \frac{\pi D^2}{4}$$

$$I = \frac{BH^3}{12}$$

$$J = \frac{BH(B^2 + H^2)}{12}$$

$$A = BH$$

WHERE I = MOMENT OF INERTIA

J = POLAR MOMENT OF INERTIA

A = AREA OF SECTION

Fig. 17-10. Sections.

```
400 PRINT"POLAR MOMENT OF INERTIA=";J
410 PRINT"MOMENT OF INERTIA=";I
420 PRINT"AREA OF SECTION=";A
430 PRINT
440 PRINT"FOR NEXT SECTION TYPE GO, IF NOT"
450 PRINT"TYPE NO"
460 INPUT L$
470 IF L$="GO" THEN 510
480 IF L$="NO" THEN 530
490 PRINT"INVALID RESPONSE"
500 GOTO 440
510 PRINT
520 GOTO 40
530 PRINT"SECTIONS SAY GOOD-BYE"
540 END
```

SERIES IMPEDANCE

```
10 REM THIS PROGRAM COMPUTES THE IMPEDANCE OF
20 REM A SERIES CIRCUIT, INVOLVING RESISTANCE,
30 REM CAPACITANCE AND INDUCTANCE. IT IS ASSUMED
40 REM THAT ALL TRIG FUNCTIONS ARE IN THE
50 REM RADIAN MODE
60 PRINT "CIRCUITS AVAILABLE ARE; RL(1), RC(2), LC(3) AND LCR(4)"
70 PRINT "ENTER THE NUMBER THAT REPRESENTS THE CIRCUIT DE-
SIRED"
80 INPUT X
90 ON X GOTO 100, 180, 260, 400
100 GOSUB 570
110 PRINT "R(OHMS), L(HENRIES) AND F(HERTZ)"
120 INPUT R,L,F
130 GOSUB 590
140 LET Z=SQR(R↑2+R1↑2)
150 LET P=ATN(R1/R)
160 GOSUB 630
170 GOTO 480
180 GOSUB 570
190 PRINT "R(OHMS), C(MFDS) AND F(HERTZ)"
200 INPUT R,C,F
210 GOSUB 610
220 LET Z=SQR(R↑2+R2↑2)
230 LET P=ATN(−R2/R)
240 GOSUB 630
250 GOTO 480
260 GOSUB 570
270 PRINT "L(HENRIES), C(MFDS) AND F(HERTZ)"
280 INPUT L,C,F
290 GOSUB 590
300 GOSUB 610
310 LET Z=ABS(R1−R2)
320 IF R1=R2 THEN 360
330 IF R1>R2 THEN 380
340 LET P=90
350 GOTO 480
360 LET P=0
370 GOTO 480
```

177

```
390 LET P=-90
390 GOTO 480
400 GOSUB 570
410 PRINT "L(HENRIES), C(MFDS), R(OHMS) AND F(HERTZ)"
420 INPUT L,C,R,F
430 GOSUB 590
440 GOSUB 610
450 LET Z=SQR(R↑2+(R1-R2)↑2)
460 LET P=ATN((R1-R2)/R)
470 GOSUB 630
480 PRINT "IMPEDANCE Z=";Z;" OHMS"
490 PRINT "PHASE ANGLE=";P;" DEGREES"
500 PRINT
510 PRINT "TO CONTINUE TYPE Y, IF NOT TYPE N"
520 INPUT Q$
530 IF Q$="Y" THEN 550
540 STOP
550 PRINT
560 GOTO 60
570 PRINT "ENTER CIRCUIT PARAMETERS"
580 RETURN
590 LET R1=6.28318*F*L
600 RETURN
610 LET R2=1E06/(6.28318*F*C)
620 RETURN
630 LET P=(P*180)/3.14159
640 RETURN
650 END
```

SPHERICAL/CARTESIAN COORDINATES

The spherical or polar coordinate system allows the location of a point in space to be specified in terms of the radius of a sphere and two angles.

The circular coordinate system is also called the polar coordinate system and uses the radius of a circle and one angle. The cartesian coordinate system uses the usual x, y or x, y, z system of location. Examples are: 50 kilometers northwest (polar) and 35 kilometers north by 35 kilometers west (cartesian).

Sometimes problems are presented in one form and can be best solved in the other. This sample program allows you to convert from one form to the other. See Fig. 17-11.

```
10 REM THIS PROGRAM CONVERTS SPHERICAL TO
20 REM CARTESIAN COORDINATES AND THE REVERSE
30 PRINT "ENTER S FOR SPHERICAL TO CARTESIAN"
40 PRINT "OR C FOR CARTESIAN TO SPHERICAL"
50 INPUT A$
60 IF A$="S" THEN 100
70 IF A$="C" THEN 250
80 PRINT "INVALID COMMAND"
90 GOTO 30
100 GOSUB 400
110 PRINT
```

```
120 PRINT "ENTER MAGNITUDE, LONGITUDE AND CO-LATITUDE"
130 INPUT M,L,C
140 IF L=0 THEN 170
150 LET L=(L*3.14159)/180
160 LET C=(C*3.14159)/180
170 LET X=M*SIN(C)*COS(L)
180 LET Y=M*SIN(C)*SIN(L)
190 LET Z=M*COS(C)
200 PRINT "CARTESIAN COORDINATES ARE:—"
210 PRINT "X=";X
220 PRINT "Y=";Y
230 PRINT "Z=";Z
240 GOTO 500
250 GOSUB 400
260 PRINT
270 PRINT "X,Y AND Z"
280 INPUT X,Y,Z
290 LET M=SQR(X↑2+Y↑2+Z↑2)
300 LET L=ATN(Y/X)
310 LET C=ACOS(Z/SQR(X↑2+Y↑2+Z↑2))
320 IF L=0 THEN 350
330 LET L=(L*180)/3.14159
340 LET C=(C*180)/3.14159
350 PRINT "SPHERICAL COORDINATES ARE :—"
360 PRINT "MAGNITUDE=";M
370 PRINT "CO-LATITUDE=";C
380 PRINT "LONGITUDE=";L
390 GOTO 500
400 PRINT "ENTER DEG FOR DEGREES AND RAD FOR RADIAN MODE"
410 INPUT A$
420 IF A$="DEG" THEN 460
430 IF A$="RAD" THEN 480
440 PRINT "INVALID RESPONSE"
450 GOTO 400
460 LET L=1
470 GOTO 490
480 LET L=0
490 RETURN
500 PRINT
510 PRINT "FOR NEXT CONVERSION TYPE GO, TO STOP"
520 PRINT "TYPE NO"
530 INPUT A$
540 IF A$="GO" THEN 580
550 IF A ="NO" THEN 600
560 PRINT "INVALID COMMAND"
570 GOTO 510
580 PRINT
590 GOTO 30
600 PRINT "COORDINATES SAY GOOD-BYE"
610 END
```

VOLUME OF COMMON SHAPES

The volume of common shapes are illustrated in Fig. 17-12.

```
10 REM THIS PROGRAM COMPUTES THE
```

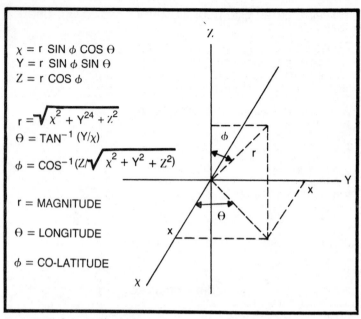

$\chi = r \sin \phi \cos \theta$
$Y = r \sin \phi \sin \theta$
$Z = r \cos \phi$

$r = \sqrt{\chi^2 + Y^{24} + \chi^2}$
$\theta = \tan^{-1}(Y/\chi)$
$\phi = \cos^{-1}(Z/\sqrt{\chi^2 + Y^2 + Z^2})$

r = MAGNITUDE

θ = LONGITUDE

ϕ = CO-LATITUDE

Fig. 17-11. Spherical/cartesian.

```
20 REM VOLUME OF COMMON SHAPES
30 PRINT "TYPE 1 FOR LISTING OF SHAPES, 0 to START"
31 INPUT C
40 IF C = 0 THEN 110
50 PRINT "OPTIONS ARE AS FOLLOWS:"
60 PRINT "(1) CUBE"
70 PRINT "(2) RECTANGULAR PRISM"
80 PRINT "(3) SPHERE"
90 PRINT "(4) CYLINDER"
100 PRINT "(5) CONE"
110 PRINT "ENTER THE NUMBER REPRESENTING THE SHAPE"
120 INPUT C
130 ON C GOSUB 150,190,230,270,310
140 PRINT "THE VOLUME IS ";X
145 GOTO 350
150 PRINT "LENGTH OF SIDE"
160 INPUT A
170 LET X = A*A*A
180 RETURN
190 PRINT "ENTER HEIGHT, WIDTH, AND LENGTH"
200 INPUT H,W,L
210 LET X = L*W*H
220 RETURN
230 PRINT "ENTER RADIUS"
240 INPUT R
250 LET X = (3.14159*R*R*R*4)/3
260 RETURN
270 PRINT "ENTER RADIUS AND HEIGHT"
```

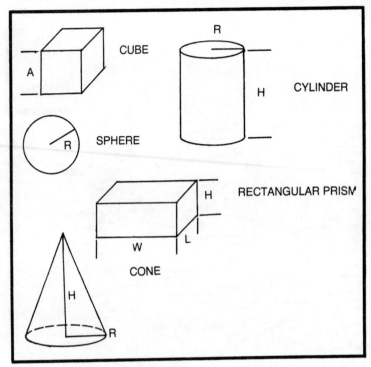

Fig. 17-12. Volume of common shapes.

```
280 INPUT R,H
290 LET X = 3.14159*H*R*R
300 RETURN
310 PRINT "ENTER RADIUS OF BASE AND HEIGHT"
320 INPUT R,H
330 LET X = (3.14159*H*R*R)/3
340 RETURN
350 PRINT "TO CONTINUE TYPE 1, TO STOP TYPE 0"
360 INPUT C
370 IF C = 1 THEN 390
380 STOP
390 PRINT
400 GOTO 30
410 END
```

Index